Wade and Shoreline Fishing

the Potomac River for Smallmouth Bass

Chain Bridge to Harpers Ferry

By Steve Moore

*The author extends a special thanks to the many members of the **Potomac River Smallmouth Club** and the **New Horizon Bass Anglers** who took the time to fact check this book and provide additional perspectives.*

Steve Moore - The SwitchFisher
Fishing the Rose River deep in the Shenandoah

Steve is an avid, hard-core, terminally addicted fisherman. He was ruined for life when his father introduced him to the sport at the age of 7 while living in Norway as a result of military duty. Chasing trout on mountain streams left an enduring imprint and drive to find new water… something that tortures Steve to this day.

Of course, this was preordained since Steve's father was fishing in a local bass tournament on the morning he was born. He claims to have had permission to go, but Steve's mother does not remember the actual facts matching that story. The point that he won a nice Shakespeare reel did nothing to mitigate the trouble he was in upon his return.

Copyright Calibrated Consulting, Inc, 2010

Exclusive of underlying Government Maps (USGS, National Park Service, Fairfax and Montgomery County), extracts from federal, state and county regulations, other public domain material and the content of the Guide chapter extracted from websites owned by the three Guides profiled that was either quoted or paraphrased.

Published by Calibrated Consulting, Inc
ISBN: 978-0-9823962-5-4 (0-9823962-5-2)
Feedback: feedback@catchguide.com

The book is dedicated to my two best fishing buddies - my wife, Donna, and my son, Chris - who tolerate, support and participate in my fishing addiction… mostly to keep an eye on me.

Table of Contents

Introduction

This is the second CatchGuide in the series that began with the guide to the North Branch of the Potomac. As I did for those 30 miles of river, I want to provide an equally detailed, focused perspective on this fantastic 57 mile section of one of the best, yet most underrated, smallmouth rivers on the East Coast.

Other Potomac books assume you have a boat; I don't. This entire book is dedicated to guiding you to locations where you can wade or fish from the shore. I include 32 named chapters that discuss the major access points in Virginia, Maryland and West Virginia. Many of these contain additional information on minor access points within the same area; expanding the total geographic coverage dramatically. *This book is "internet aware" and includes over 200 GPS coordinates useable in Google Maps for precise directions*. In fact, you should use the satellite picture for a birds-eye view of each location. You could spend years fishing all these different places! In the spirit of full disclosure, I visited and put my trained fisherman's eye on every location discussed in this book. However, for the small number of additional access points I discovered while doing my research, I relied on advice from others to fill in the gaps.

If you have a boat or want additional information about fishing the Potomac, you should read Ken Penrod's critically acclaimed *Fishing the Upper Potomac River.* Even though it was written in 1989, the geography of the river remains the same, his advice is timeless and the book provides a good history lesson overlaid on very specific detail regarding the best spots on the river.

Beyond stale words in print, I strongly recommend you join a vibrant and active angler's organization such as the Potomac River Smallmouth Club. That group has been providing peer-to-peer advice since 1988. Visit them at www.prsc.org. Another good club is the New Horizon Bass Anglers with their focus on youth (www.nhbayouthfoundation.org)

Given that a picture is worth a 1,000 words, I'll provide many of them. I hope that you find the pictures to be the most informative aspect of the book. I don't know about you, but I have spent hours driving to places that proved to be a disappointment. If I had had the opportunity to look at the water first via pictures, I would have gone someplace else.

I hope you find this CatchGuide helpful, and wish you the best of luck on the river.

Steve Moore

General Perspective on the Potomac

The Chesapeake and Ohio Canal National Historical Park stretches north for 184.5 miles from Georgetown to Cumberland, Maryland; more fishing than any single person could master in a lifetime! This CatchGuide covers 57.3 miles, less than a third of the total, between the Chain Bridge in the District of Columbia and the lip of Dam 3 at Harpers Ferry.

Given the proximity to the Washington Metropolitan area, the Potomac is a popular fishing destination for the many smallmouth bass fanatics who live within an hour's drive. The incorrect assumption that many of them make is that the only way to find good fishing on the river is to use canoes, kayaks and boats. The reality is that there are plenty of places to fish this wonderful river reachable using shoe leather.

In fact, the best areas for wading are the two bookends of the river. The areas between Lock 7 and Seneca Breaks as well as Harpers Ferry downstream through the Brunswick campground are ideal sections for the foot-mobile angler. Between the bookends, the river offers plenty of hotspots such as Lander and Point of Rocks. As a general statement, all you need to do to find fishing is to go up or downstream; it won't be long before you see a good spot.

If you prefer to fish from the shore, your options expand to include the deeper areas that lie between the bookends. The only limiting factor on your day will be the density of the vegetation hanging off of the steep bank propping up the towpath as you bushwhack your way to the shoreline.

Whether you wade or fish from the shoreline, you are only a cast away from hooking into many massive smallmouth bass that fin serenely in the channels or huddle behind rocks looking for an easy meal. Thankfully, the Potomac has not been the victim of the drastic fish kills that plagued the Shenandoah in recent years. The population of "beasts" remains intact.

Whether you fish from the shore or wade, a good "fishing bike" provides a tremendous mobility advantage. The C&O Canal NHP provides miles of well maintained, smooth roadway that runs within sight of the river for much of its length. A bike allows you to move rapidly between locations – no wasted time walking!

A quick comment is appropriate here on the GPS coordinates included in each section. If you put them into Google Maps, be sure and look for the GREEN arrow and not the RED arrow. Google tends to jump to a regional feature and shows it using the RED arrow. You may have to zoom out to see the GREEN arrow that marks the actual location.

Rules and Regulations

If you are going to fish on the Potomac River, you must read this section!

There are some tricky rules and regulations that, if you remain blissfully unaware of them, you could find yourself in unexpected trouble. As with all laws, ignorance is no excuse.

I need to include the required and obvious **liability disclaimer** at this point. I am not a lawyer. I'm a fisherman. While I coordinated this chapter to confirm accuracy with a senior representative of the Enforcement Division of the C&O Canal NHP system and different individuals in the Fairfax County government, policies can change faster than this book can be republished. You and you alone are solely responsible for correctly understanding and interpreting all laws and regulations that apply to the Potomac. It is your obligation to stay current on changes. Therefore, *I, as well as the publisher and, by extension, the government representatives, disclaim all liability associated with your interpretation and application of not only the material in this chapter but, as stated in the overall liability disclaimer, everything in this book.* While I believe this book is accurate and current as of the date of publication, the individuals and organizations listed above shall not be held liable for misleading or incorrect information. If you have questions, I recommend you give the Park a call prior to visiting. We welcome you to send an e-mail to feedback@catchguide.com if you discover any errors or inaccuracies.

Common Sense

Before getting into the details of the regulations, there are common sense rules that should be obvious to anyone who approaches a river as powerful as the Potomac. The most important rule is that "If you have a doubt, then there is no doubt." If your gut is telling you that something is risky, then it probably is. Listen to your inner voice!

The section of the Potomac discussed in this book contains two areas that are dangerous beyond the inherent risk associated with a river whose levels can rise abruptly and violently after a significant rainfall. These are the Little Falls Dam section and the entire Great Falls Park. Of the two, the Great Falls area, from either the Virginia and Maryland shore, is the more dangerous venue and is exceptionally hazardous.

If you fish from the shore or attempt to wade in Great Falls or in/near the Mather Gorge, you will probably die. Every year a significant number of people lose their lives doing stupid things at the edge of the water.

All you need to do is look at the picture and ask yourself, "Why would anyone take a chance in an area that is so obviously hazardous?" Sadly, people do. Please exercise good judgment and make sure that neither you nor your loved ones leave this world early as a result of a false step on a slippery rock.

Beyond the obvious danger associated with these two locations, the Potomac River can be hazardous anywhere depending on the water levels and the volume of flow. Nominally, the Potomac is at "normal" levels for wading when the gage reading at Point of Rocks is below 2.0 feet or Little Falls is below 3.5 feet. However, you cannot rely on that as the absolute arbiter of safety. Granted, the lower it goes as the weather heats up and the river drops to its summer pool levels, the safer it becomes. But a general assertion of safety does not apply equally across a 50 mile stretch of river. In fact, just like politics, safety is local. As you fish in the river, you must be aware of your immediate surroundings. The rocks are slippery, there are deep sections that will surprise you when you step forward in water that may be murky and, of course, the shoreline can be equally challenging with steep banks, poison ivy and assorted snakes. For all of these reasons, I strongly recommend that when you fish in the Potomac, you extend the Maryland State regulation that requires boaters to wear a personal flotation device between November 15 and May 15 and always wear one - especially if you do not know how to swim or are wearing waders. Finally, use a wading staff to test footing and depth as you move in the river.

Here is the general guidance from the Maryland DNR on wading in the Potomac:

> "Wading or swimming should not be attempted when the river level is at the caution or danger level or when the Potomac River Advisory is in effect. Slippery footing plus the increased velocity of the current can easily cause a life threatening situation. Strong currents exist in the Upper Potomac River that can drag you under. Wading in the waters around Great Falls is prohibited.

> At *ANY* river level **Personal Flotation Devices** (Life Jackets) are recommended while on, in, or near the water. Drownings have occurred when people walking on rocks slipped and fell into the water. Wading in the river without a life jacket is dangerous. Anglers should be aware that chest waders can fill with water and pull them under. Chest waders should be tied snugly around the chest to help prevent this. Again, a life jacket should be worn. There are several designs that allow free movement of the arms."

If you are sensitive to poison ivy, you should use a sunscreen that includes protection against the toxic oils of this plant. I use IVY DRY Defense Protective Lotion and find it to be very effective. In addition, when I leave the water, I rub IVAREST poison ivy cleansing foam on my exposed skin as well as roll up my trousers and put it on my lower legs. Poison ivy oils can penetrate wet fabric easily. Finally, when I get home, I use the CVS pharmacy brand poison ivy soap as the final layer of defense.

Do not leave valuables in your vehicle; especially if they are visible. The Park Service posts numerous signs reminding visitors of this simple protective measure, but every year thieves break into cars in the parking areas.

If you use your bike to move along the towpath to get to some of the areas described in this book, be sure to lock your bike when you leave it to go to the river.

Federal Regulations

The first thing to understand is where different regulations apply. The National Park Service in the National Capital Region owns responsibility for the Chesapeake and Ohio Canal National Historic Park (C&O Canal NHP). The state of Maryland owns and has jurisdiction over the river upstream from the boundary with the District of Columbia just north of the Chain Bridge as well as controls its own State parkland that is adjacent to the C&O Canal NHP. Inside the District of Columbia, the District controls the river. In addition to Maryland State parks, there are several Montgomery County Parks that abut the C&O Canal NHP, and the County has jurisdiction over that land.

Given this division of responsibility, the National Park Service does not establish any of the regulations associated with fishing such as catch and release, creel limits, tackle restrictions or other limitations on what you can do while on Maryland State or District property (i.e. the river). The National Park system's jurisdiction is limited to the explicit boundaries of the C&O Canal NHP. The boundary between federal and Maryland state property is the mean high water level mark. The Park provides Rangers, establishes the rules and regulations, and has the authority to enforce those laws on federal property.

As a side note, I recommend that if you encounter a Ranger -- and you will see them slowly creeping up and down the towpath in white vehicles -- you stop and chat with them as many can give you good guidance on current fishing and river conditions that will make your visit more successful.

In addition to the C&O Canal NHP, the National Capital Region has jurisdiction over the George Washington Memorial Parkway. As anglers, we care about that because the Parkway includes Turkey Run Park; a key access point on the Virginia side of the Potomac below the American Legion Bridge. The federal property ends at the boundary where the George Washington Memorial Parkway intersects I-495 in the north and at the low water mark with the river (Virginia and Maryland negotiated the low water mark as the boundary between the states). With the exception of the Virginia section of the Great Falls Park, the Virginia riverbank contains a mix of private, State and County controlled land upstream from the American Legion Bridge. Beyond Great Falls, there is no federally managed property adjacent to the river in Virginia until you reach Harpers Ferry.

In Maryland, the C&O Canal NHP extends the entire length of the river from Chain Bridge all the way up to and beyond Harpers Ferry.

The governing regulation can be found in 36 CFR Ch. 1 (7-1-01 edition).

You can find a current copy of this regulation on the National Park Service website (www.nps.gov/nama/planyourvisit/permits.htm).

Here is the section that establishes the regulatory framework for the Potomac covered in this book (I put the key items in "bold" text. This text is not in bold in the original regulation):

> § 7.96 National Capital Region.
>
> (a) *Applicability of regulations.* This section **applies to all park areas administered by National Capital Region** in the District of Columbia and in Arlington, **Fairfax**, Loudoun, Prince William, and Stafford Counties and the City of Alexandria in Virginia and Prince Georges, Charles, Anne Arundel, and **Montgomery Counties** in Maryland and to other federal reservations in the environs of the District of Columbia, policed with the approval or concurrence of the head of the agency having jurisdiction or control over such reservations, pursuant to the provisions of the act of March 17, 1948 (62 Stat. 81).

Basically, what this says is that the regulations in subsequent paragraphs are applicable to the entire extent of the C&O Canal NHP up to the northern boundary of Montgomery County as well as to the George Washington Memorial Parkway that sits across the river in Fairfax County.

Here are the specific sections that govern your activity on federal property (again, I bolded key text):

> (d) *Fishing.* Unless otherwise designated, **fishing** in a manner authorized **under applicable State law** is **allowed**.
>
> (e) *Swimming.* Bathing, swimming or wading in any fountain or pool except where officially authorized is prohibited. Bathing, swimming or **wading** in the Tidal Basin, the Chesapeake and Ohio Canal, or Rock Creek, **or entering from other areas covered by this section the Potomac River**, Anacostia River, Washington Channel or Georgetown Channel, except for the purpose of saving a drowning person, **is prohibited**.

Section 7.96(d) confirms that Maryland regulations apply to fishing in the Potomac River. Maryland does not prohibit wading while fishing. In fact, Maryland has its own view, specifically authorizing fishing/wading with a few constraints, which I discuss in the next section.

Section 7.96(e) prohibits swimming, bathing and wading and the word "or" connects those activities to entering the Potomac River from Park property. The boundary between the Park and Maryland is the mean high water mark with the river rising and falling with the weather.

The interpretation of these two sections matters because there are a number of access points that have prominent "No Wading" signs displayed. Does wading include fishing or is it separate?

I discussed this with the Chief Ranger of the C&O Canal NHP and he told me that Maryland law prevails. Since Maryland law defines fishing as a different activity than wading and section 7.96(d) defers to state law regarding fishing, the C&O Canal NHP permits to anglers to wade while fishing. Since this book will be in print for years and regulations will evolve, I recommend that you take one additional step to ensure that you fall in the "fishing" category. A close read of section 7.96(e) reveals that there are three things that the Park wants to constrain; swimming, bathing, and wading. Typically, individuals engaged those activities do not do them while wearing a PFD. Therefore, if you wear a PFD, you push yourself farther into the fishing category. Besides, in the areas specifically called out with the signs, it's the prudent and safe thing to do.

Maryland State Regulations

In addition to the generic guidance from Maryland quoted in the common sense section, there are specific restrictions associated with the more dangerous areas of the Potomac. These are captured in Title 08 (Department of Natural Resources), Subtitle 06 (Recreational Water Uses), Chapter 01 (Potomac River Safety) of the Maryland code.

Specifically, section 03 establishes two special regulatory zones:

*Zone A. A person may not enter the Potomac River for the purpose of **recreational use** in that portion of the Potomac River beginning 200 yards above the crest of Aqueduct Intake Dam (Great Falls) and extending downstream to the base of Stubblefield Falls.*

*Zone B. A person may not enter the Potomac River for the purpose of **recreational use** in that portion of the Potomac River beginning 100 yards above the crest of Dam No. 1 (Brookmont Dam) and extending downstream to the western Maryland and District of Columbia boundary line.*

The law goes on to further define "recreational use" in section 08.06.01.02 and makes an exception for fishing (my bold):

(2) Recreational Use.
    (a) "Recreational use" means activities on the Potomac River, including swimming, bathing, wading, diving, tubing, rafting, and other uses involving contact with the water.
    (b) "Recreational use" does not include:
        (i) Boating, if each person involved is wearing the U.S. Coast Guard approved flotation device required by law or regulation;
        (ii) Fishing, when a U.S. Coast Guard approved personal flotation device is worn;
        (iii) Life-saving efforts;
        (iv) Swimming or wading as part of a training course having the prior written approval of the Department of Natural Resources or U.S. Park Service.

The bottom line is that if you fish in the two special zones, you must wear a PFD.

One final point is that the above regulation is in conflict with the quote I pulled from the Maryland DNR publication that indicated "Wading in the waters around Great Falls is prohibited." I was unable to find that in a state law, but fully agree that it should be a law. It may exist... buried in the code somewhere.

It is this section of Maryland law, until changed or reinterpreted, that provides the opportunity for anglers to wade while fishing in compliance with the federal regulation:

> (d) *Fishing*. Unless otherwise designated, **fishing** in a manner authorized **under applicable State law** is **allowed**.

Separate and distinct from 08.06.01, is another Maryland rule that requires individuals who are boating, including tubers, to wear a personal flotation device between November 15 and May 15.

Fairfax County and Northern Virginia Regional Park Regulations

Fairfax County and the Northern Virginia Regional Park Authority adopted the same set of regulatory guidance in joint Park Authority Regulations (for a list see appendix 7 of the Park policy manual) covering their properties. The manual includes a prohibition on wading in rivers adjacent to their parks (my bold).

§1.21 Swimming, Bathing and Wading
Swimming, bathing and **wading are prohibited** in bodies of water, to include, but not limited to, streams, **rivers**, ponds or lakes, within or adjacent to a park without the express written permission of the Park Authority. Swimming, bathing and wading in a park are permitted only in water facilities established by the Park Authority for such purposes and only during posted hours of operation.

The problem is that neither Fairfax County nor Virginia has any jurisdiction over the river since it is actually in Maryland. The formal border between the two states is the low water mark on the Virginia side. They agreed with my assessment and Fairfax quoted the problem with "Naked Ned" as an example of their inability to enforce this regulation once an individual is beyond the border. "Naked Ned" is an eccentric individual who wears what he was born in and wades, making rock weirs, in the vicinity of Stubblefield Falls. Virginia authorities cannot arrest him for indecent exposure as long as he stays in the river.

Neither organization wants to change the written language because of concerns that if they post a sign that permits anglers to wade, everyone will assume they can; resulting in a potential increase in drowning as small children and others who may not be as situationally aware as an angler enter the water. They recognize that they do not have authority beyond the Virginia State boundary. As this book goes to press, the Fairfax County Park system is considering posting signs at river access points warning anglers that they are about to enter Maryland and that they do so at their own risk; an indication that the Park recognizes Maryland's authority over the river.

Another aspect that factors into this mess is that the Potomac River has been designated as a navigable river by both the Army Corps of Engineers and by a Virginia State Act. The public has the right to use the river up to the "ordinary high water mark"; something that has been affirmed by numerous Supreme Court decisions. For more information, visit the National Rivers website at www.nationalrivers.org/us-law-public.htm.

All my discussion of the river adjacent to these properties assumes you found a legal way to get there. So, I leave it up to you on how you interpret the restriction/regulation discussed above and deal with it.

Note that the Maryland State law that requires anglers to wear a PFD in certain sections of the river is totally valid and fully enforceable by Maryland.

Other Regulations

When you drive into any of the Parks discussed in this book, pay attention to whether there is a gate across the road. If there is, the typical Park hours will run from early morning to sunset. Look for a sign near the gate with the parks operating hours. Typically, all of the gates close at sunset. You do not want to be caught on the wrong side of the gate at the end of the day.

You can only ride your bike on the towpath, not the trails.

If biking, you must wear a helmet and your bike must have a bell. You should ring the bell as you overtake hikers to warn them of your approach. The last thing you want to do is have a hiker make an abrupt turn at the wrong time. The speed limit for bikes is 15 mph.

The Park allows camping in different locations along the 184 miles of the park including 30 hiker-biker spots. The campgrounds are typically first come, first served and feature a chemical toilet, picnic table, grill and water.

Finally, before I end this chapter, I need to revisit the liability disclaimer and make a comment about trespass. This information is as accurate as I can make it, but it is your responsibility to know, understand and apply the law to your specific situation. Things may change more rapidly than this book can be updated and, accordingly, the author, the publisher and anyone else or other organization that provided input to this book disclaims responsibility for any decision you make or any outcome of your decisions as a result of relying on this information.

In terms of trespass, laws change and, beyond that, property changes hands frequently. Nothing in this book is intended to encourage you to violate any trespass laws. All of us must respect private property rights and you are responsible for decisions you make, based on the situation that exists at the time, to ensure your actions are legal.

Water Volume / Flow – THE key to success

Knowledge of current river conditions will save you a significant amount of frustration and heartache. The quality of the fishing comes and goes with both the amount and clarity of the water. If you know what to look for and where to check to determine the current conditions, you will avoid wasted treks in the grinding traffic around the beltway only to discover an unfishable situation. This chapter identifies the two primary USGS gages, Point of Rocks and Little Falls, that monitor conditions and provides guidance on how to interpret them.

As a general statement, to be fishable, the water flow (measured in cubic feet per second – "cfs" or gage height in feet) must be below the minimum level to make whitewater addicts happy. There is a great website – www.americanwhitewater.org – the kayak crowd uses to determine put-in and take-out points and share conditions. The website has real-time river flow status color-coded based on a kayaker's point of view for different sections of the river:

State Summary

Level Legend: Running Below Minimum Recommended Flow Above Maximum Recommended Flow Unknown
Descriptions of reaches with River Name in bold have been verified by a regional StreamTeam member.

State	River Name/Section	Class	Level		Rel. Level	Updated
MD	Anacostia, Northwest Branch— US Rte 29 to Riggs Road	I-III(V+)	16 cfs		low	3/10 9:30
MD	Antietam Creek— 1) Upper: Oak Bridge to Hwy 68	I-II	2.58 feet		low	3/10 9:00
MD	Antietam Creek— 2) Hwy 68 to Potomac River	I-II	2.58 ft		med	3/10 9:00
MD	Bear Creek— U.S. 219 to Youghiogheny River at Friendsville	IV	44 cfs		low	3/10 9:30 ⚠

When you click on an entry, the website provides expanded guidance on minimum/maximum whitewater levels. In the case shown below, the range that would make the trip worthwhile for a kayaker is between 2.8 and 6.8 feet with the current reading being 4.98 ft. For fishing, you do not want to be swept away, so you want the gage to be close to or below the minimum before you go fishing.

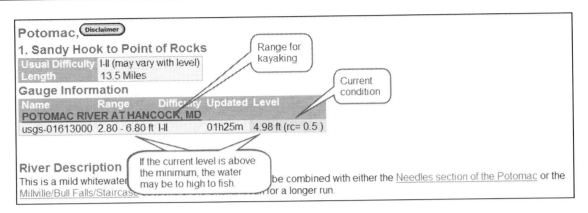

It is important to point out that the minimum whitewater level may still be above the maximum fishing level, so be careful. If you fish the river below the minimum level, you will probably not have kayakers floating over the great hole you just started to work.

Beyond the whitewater measurements, the river does have a set of conditions, specific to each gage, which defines "normal", "caution" and "danger." The commonly accepted guidance for "wadeability" is that the gages must be below the upper range of what is considered normal. It's certainly okay for the level to be lower, but you need to be wary if it is much higher than normal. That's where the decision becomes conditional on the specific part of the river you intend to fish and the specific place where you enter from the shore. By fishing where the river broadens, the volume of water will spread over a greater area, resulting in a shallower average depth and mitigate the impact of higher readings. You certainly do not want to put your foot in the water anyplace where the river compresses when the flow is high. Finally, recognize that higher flows typically bring additional silt into the water column. The murkier the water becomes, the more difficult it will be to have a successful day. So even if you can fish from the shore on a high water day, the water may be cloudy and limit the number of fish that view or sense the presence of your lure.

Each of the two gages provides water measurements of both cubic feet per second and gage height in feet. The single metric that most anglers use is the gage height in feet and I will use that in this book. The height in feet is available as either the mean or the median. Either of these is fine if you are looking at the gage reading to decide if you want to go fishing today or tomorrow. If you are looking farther into the future and planning a significant trip, there is a critical difference between these two statistics.

The mean is the average of all the readings. The median is the middle reading. For example, if there were 11 measures of the gage height and they were placed in ascending order, the median would be the value that occurred in the sixth place since there would be five higher measures and five lower measures surrounding it. While you can use either measurement to assess real-time conditions on the river, I prefer to use the median for planning. The reason is that a significant weather event can produce a drastically abnormal high or low spike and that single number will impact the value of the mean.

Whereas, if you use the median, that dramatic high or low would just be one more value in the ordered sequence of which the middle value is the median. In short, relying on the median minimizes the impact of huge swings based on the weather.

Harpers Ferry to Nolands Landing

The Point of Rocks gage is the gage that covers this section although many anglers use this to assess the fishability of the entire river. However, purists recognize that since the Point of Rocks gage is upstream of the mouth of the Monocacy River, it does not accurately portray the situation downstream since it will not account for the added volume contributed by the Monocacy.

The generally accepted maximum gage reading for "normal" volume at the Point of Rocks gage is 2.0 feet. Just to be clear, 2.0 feet is the lower limit of the "caution" level with the entire normal range being between 0.7 and 2.0 feet. The lower the reading; the better the wading. My personal preference is to fish when the gage reading is below 1.7.

Here is a table that shows the median height in feet at the Point of Rocks gage over the last 8 years. See the chapter on water flows and gage heights at the back of the book for the average and/or median height and flow by day.

Point of Rocks - Average of Median for 8 years of record											
	Jan	Feb	Mar	Apr	May	Jun	Jul	Aug	Sep	Oct	Nov	Dec
Avg	3.31	3.13	4.55	4.34	3.60	2.25	1.83	1.61	1.79	2.15	3.19	3.45

The general conclusion from the eight year average is that the water is generally under control between late June and October. The rainy months of the spring have the most potential for danger and dictate that you check the gage and use caution prior to entering the river. Don't plan your once-in-a-lifetime trip to the Potomac in March or April!

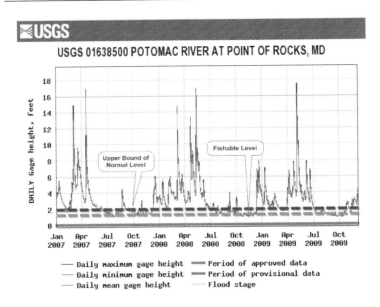

USGS 01638500 POTOMAC RIVER AT POINT OF ROCKS, MD

The graph to the left shows the daily flows for the period January 2007 through December 2009 to give you a visual picture of the typical cycle.

Note how quickly the flow can spike from safe to life threatening.

Each of the sharp highs has a long-term impact on the mean value.

The depressing fact is that the river is unfishable for wading anglers most of the year.

Monocacy River to Chain Bridge

The Little Falls gage is the gage that covers this section. The Little Falls gage reflects the impact of all the additional stream flows into the river from Monocacy downstream.

The generally accepted maximum gage reading for normal volume at the Little Falls gage is 3.5 feet. Just to be clear, 3.5 feet is the lower limit of the "caution" level with the entire normal range being between 2.9 and 3.5 feet. The lower the reading, the better the wading - with my personal preference is to fish when the gage is below 3.1 feet with the optimum level below 2.9. I advise caution above 3.1 even though it is within the normal range.

Here is a table that shows the median height at the Little Falls gage over the last 8 years. See the chapters on water flows and gage heights at the back of the book for the average and/or median height and flow by day.

Little Falls - Average of Median for 8 years of record											
	Jan	Feb	Mar	Apr	May	Jun	Jul	Aug	Sep	Oct	Nov	Dec
Avg	4.00	3.92	4.53	4.49	4.10	3.47	3.23	2.92	2.82	3.27	3.87	4.00

The general conclusion from the eight year average is different from the one we reached for the Point of Rocks gage; the water levels are generally under control between late July and October. The rainy months of the spring have the most potential for danger and dictate that you check the gage and use caution prior to entering the river.

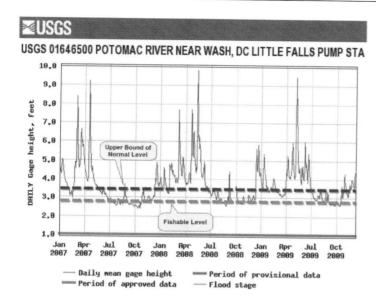

USGS

USGS 01646500 POTOMAC RIVER NEAR WASH, DC LITTLE FALLS PUMP STA

The graph to the left shows the daily flows for the period January 2007 through December 2009 to give you a visual picture of the typical cycle.

This shows that the river downstream from Monocacy has more "normal" wadeable days than upriver.

The bottom line is that water level and clarity dictate how successful any particular trip will be. Higher flows usually translate to murky water as the additional volume flushes significant amounts of mud and silt into the river. You do not want to even think about entering the river if the water levels exceed the upper boundary of the normal range. You may still be able to fish from the shore depending on the clarity at that particular location.

As a final point, the table below shows the average difference in height between the Little Falls and Point of Rocks gages. If you only have time to check one, this will give you a rough idea of the reading on the other gage. It's interesting to see that in periods of high flow, such as the spring, there is very little difference between the two gages; emphasizing the extreme danger associated with the river during high water events. In short, if it's blown out in one place, it's blown out everyplace.

Average of the difference in the median gage height (Little Falls - Point of Rocks)											
Jan	Feb	Mar	Apr	May	Jun	Jul	Aug	Sep	Oct	Nov	Dec
0.69	0.78	-0.02	0.15	0.51	1.22	1.40	1.30	1.03	1.13	0.68	0.55

Best Time to Fish

In a general sense, it's easy to figure out the best time to fish. All you need to do is wake up and check your pulse. If you are alive and don't have to go to work, then it is a good day to fish. Given that you are still breathing, the next thing to determine is whether that particular day is good enough to justify surviving the nightmare associated with DC traffic to reach the river.

The first thing to do is to check the relevant gage based on whether you are fishing above or below the Monocacy River. If the gage is above the normal level, abandon your plans, mow the yard, and build up some "credits" with your spouse to cash in on a better day. If the gage is within the normal range, then you are "good to go" with the caveat that you should calibrate the gage to your personal comfort level and define "normal" based on your individual capabilities.

A rapid rise in water level usually produces murky water. Therefore, even though the gage may be within the normal range, you must consider the impact of weather. If it rained recently, and the gage is still high, don't bother to go. If it rained over a week ago and the gage is still high (but within a safe range), it may be worth chancing it under the assumption that the silt has settled.

After each visit, check the gage and decide whether you felt comfortable in the water or on the shoreline at that reading.

Predictive Gages

Given the hectic lifestyles that many of us experience, it's a little naïve to think that we do not make plans. In addition to checking the weather, checking with friends, I want to have some level of guarantee that the water levels will be within the proper range before I drive out. Granted, you could check this the day before or at the last minute, but that may be too late to change plans and do something else or go to a different location.

Thankfully, the National Weather Service comes to our rescue. On their website (www.erh.noaa.gov/lwx/), they update predictive graphs to provide an estimate of what the water levels will be at different periods in the future. Obviously, these predictions will be more accurate when looking out a few days versus a month. Therefore, a few days before I hit the river, I check the graph to verify that the water level will be okay and, if not, I'll adjust my plans to do something else or go to a different place; like hit the mountain trout streams in the Shenandoah.

Here's an example for the Little Falls predictive page:

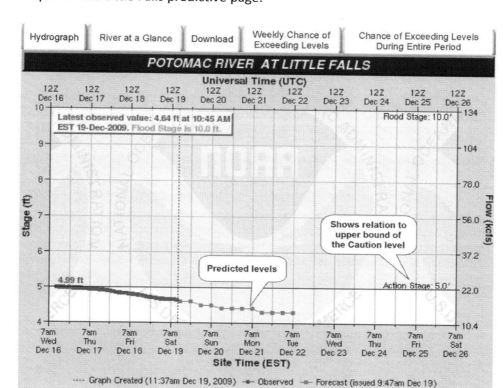

The graph shows the level in feet on the left and the flow in cubic feet per second on the right. In this case, the current level was approximately 4.7 feet on December 19th and by December 22nd; it was predicted to drop to approximately 4.4 feet.

On the same page, you can click an option to look across the entire one-month period of prediction. The site presents a graph that shows the probability of the river exceeding different levels. I do not find that graph to be as informative since I'm usually not interested in the water level over an extended period of time. I just want to know what it is going to be in the next couple of days so I can make my plans. There are other displays that show stacked bar charts of probability by week over the next month.

Water Temperature

The time frame when the water level is acceptable spans the months from June to October. Inside that window of time, water temperature controls your decision on wet wading. Given the risk of wearing chest waders, you may decide to limit your fishing to the warmest periods. That wonderful, narrow period during the summer runs from June to the end of September. A chapter at the back of the book shows the historical water temperatures for each day of the year. Here's the quick bottom line on temperature based on averages:

Days	Jan	Feb	Mar	Apr	May	Jun	Jul	Aug	Sep	Oct	Nov	Dec
Water Temperature in degrees Fahrenheit												
Mean values for each half month period for 9 years of record												
1 - 15	39.7	37.0	44.6	54.7	65.6	76.0	83.6	84.4	77.2	66.2	52.5	42.7
16 - 31	35.8	39.2	49.1	60.8	68.3	80.7	84.2	81.5	72.8	58.3	48.9	39.6
Average	37.7	38.1	46.9	57.7	67.0	78.3	83.9	82.9	75.0	64.2	49.1	41.1

In my view, the threshold of pain is 70°. Given that number, June through September are the best times to wet wade. While I certainly do not want to discourage you from fishing at other times given the natural increase in activity associated with the spring spawn as well as the late fall feeding frenzy, comfort certainly has to play into your decision. The best way to fish during the cold water times of year, assuming safe water levels, is in a boat or from the shore.

Of course, the other way to look at this is from the fish's perspective. Ken Penrod, who is the area's top expert on the Potomac River, defines "bass summer" by water temperature. Based on fish activity, summer starts water temperature hits 60° and ends when it drops below that number in the fall. Looking at the water temperature chart at the back of the book, in an average year, "bass summer" begins on April 19 and extends all the way through October 21. While this is critical information if you have a boat, it's not that useful to folks who want to wade. The reason is that the early spring is when the water levels are high and unsafe and that pushes the season farther into the "human summer" for waders. On the other hand, shoreline fishers can take advantage of the earlier start.

Beyond the issues associated with temperature and water level, you have to return to the basics of bass fishing to have a successful day. There are plenty of other books on the tactics and techniques associated with smallmouth bass fishing that address the impact of visible light, whether the barometer is rising or falling, air and water temperature, feeding patterns and all of the other quirks of nature that drive bass behavior. A discussion of those criteria would fill an additional book. If you are interested in those fine points, I recommend you pick up one of Ken Penrod's (*Pursuing River Smallmouth Bass*) or Harry Murray's (*Fly Fishing for Smallmouth Bass*) books that cover the subject much better than I could ever imagine.

Understanding the Rating System

Every fisherman looks at a body of water in a way that matches their background and compares what they see to their personal concept of "perfect." I am no different. To fully understand the comments I make in this guide, you need to understand how I evaluate water.

The tables below attempt to normalize my perspective into a common frame of reference. The key ratings are the ones related to physical fitness, the wadeability of a particular stretch, and whether spin or fly gear provides the right technical approach to catch more fish - or even whether it is feasible to fly fish at all.

In general, you can use spin gear anywhere on the river with the only issue being the choice of terminal tackle since some places limit you to a weedless presentation. Fly fishing becomes problematic in those areas where the towpath creates a steep ledge and your ability to move out into the river is limited by the depth of the water. To enjoy the entire river, you should adopt both fishing approaches and grab the rod best suited for the particular situation

The one rating that I do not include is whether fishing a particular section is dangerous. Clearly, if you try and fish in the Mather Gorge, you are totally insane. Likewise, there are other places where the water is fast, the ledges are slick, the approach involves traversing risky terrain and you may put yourself at risk if you're not careful. While I will point out the hazards that were apparent to me, for obvious reasons associated with liability, *you must be the final arbiter on whether you are comfortable fishing in a particular location and must use your common sense based on the conditions on that particular day prior to entering the water. You are solely and fully responsible for any decision you make to enter the river.*

The physical fitness rating is based on my impression of what it takes to get to the fishing area and enjoy it. Something I consider challenging may be easy for you or, on the other end of the scale, impossible based on your personal physical situation. *You should never attempt to fish in any spot where taking a step off the bank creates personal risk.* Just because I did not think a particular place was overly taxing physically may not mean much until you match your abilities with mine.

Please re-read and agree to the liability disclaimer on page 2 of the CatchGuide before you read further.

The tables below lay out the criteria:

Rating Explanations

Pressure	**Green**	Rarely see other people
	Yellow	Saw other people, but never felt pressured
	Red	Popular and crowded
Scenery	**Green**	Rock ledges, interesting water
	Yellow	Flat water, broad sweep of river
	Red	Populated
Physical Fitness	**Green**	Smooth flow, easy wading, stable bottom
	Yellow	Some rock ledges, moderate water speed, wading staff advisable; minor hike
	Red	Fast water, slippery rocks, wading staff required **or** long hike to get there
Wading	**Green**	Good wading over a broad area
	Yellow	Limited opportunity to wade; restricted to shorelines or specific places
	Red	Deep water, not good for wading
Shore Fishing	**Green**	Easily fishable from shore
	Yellow	Fishable but you have to pick your spots
	Red	Poor access - steep banks
Spin Fishing	**Green**	No problems using spin gear
	Yellow	Structure may cause spinners and crankbaits to hang up or snag the bottom
	Red	Structure forces weedless approach (Texas rig, etc)

Rating Explanations

Category	Rating	Explanation
Fly Fishing	Green	Open terrain allows backcast
	Yellow	Some obstructions for backcast
	Red	No room for backcast
Canoe or Kayak Launch	Green	Access point useable by canoes or kayaks
	Yellow	Useable but requires a carry
	Red	No access to launch a canoe or kayak
Trailer Boat Launch	Green	Includes a ramp to launch a trailered boat
	Red	No ramp
Parking	Green	Formal parking area with plenty of spaces
	Yellow	Formal parking area with limited number of spaces
	Red	Park on shoulder
Regulations	Green	Catch and Release
	Red	May keep fish
Overall	Green	Always good
	Yellow	Conditions dictate
	Red	Not worth it

Overall Rating Summary

Here are my conclusions "up front." See each section for details.

	Pressure	Physical Fitness	Wading	Shore Fishing	Spin Fishing	Fly Fishing
Chain Bridge	Yellow	Red	Red	Green	Green	Yellow
Lock 6	Yellow	Red	Red	Green	Green	Yellow
Sycamore Island	Green	Red	Red	Red	Green	Red
Lock 7	Yellow	Yellow	Yellow	Green	Yellow	Green
Lock 8	Yellow	Yellow	Green	Green	Yellow	Green
Turkey Run Park	Red	Red	Green	Yellow	Yellow	Green
Lock 10	Yellow	Yellow	Red	Green	Green	Green
Scotts Run	Green	Red	Yellow	Yellow	Green	Green
Carderock	Yellow	Yellow	Yellow	Green	Green	Green
Angler's Inn	Yellow	Green	Red	Green	Green	Yellow
Great Falls	Red	Red	Red	Red	Red	Red
Riverbend Regional Park	Red	Green	Green	Green	Green	Green
Swains Lock	Red	Yellow	Yellow	Green	Green	Green
Pennyfield Lock	Yellow	Green	Green	Yellow	Green	Green
Seneca Breaks	Red	Red	Green	Green	Yellow	Green
Fraser Preserve/NoVA	Green	Red	Green	Yellow	Yellow	Green
Algonkian Regional Park	Yellow	Green	Red	Green	Green	Red
Sycamore Landing	Green	Green	Green	Yellow	Green	Green
Edwards Ferry	Yellow	Green	Yellow	Green	Green	Yellow
Bles, Mills, Goose Creek	Green	Yellow	Green	Green	Green	Green
Red Rocks Wilderness	Green	Green	Red	Green	Green	Red
Balls Bluff Battlefield	Green	Yellow	Red	Green	Green	Red
Whites Ferry	Red	Green	Yellow	Yellow	Green	Green
Dickerson	Green	Yellow	Green	Green	Green	Green
Monocacy	Yellow	Green	Yellow	Yellow	Green	Green
Nolands Ferry	Yellow	Green	Yellow	Red	Green	Green
Point of Rocks	Red	Green	Yellow	Yellow	Green	Green
Lander	Red	Green	Green	Green	Green	Green
Brunswick Campground	Green	Green	Green	Red	Green	Green
Brunswick Launch	Yellow	Yellow	Green	Yellow	Green	Green
Knoxville Falls	Red	Red	Green	Green	Green	Green
Harpers Ferry	Red	Red	Green	Green	Green	Green

Here are the remaining criteria and the overall summary rating for each location:

	Scenery	Canoe or Kayak	Trailered Boat	Parking	Regulations	Overall
Chain Bridge	Green	Red	Red	Green	Yellow	Yellow
Lock 6	Yellow	Red	Red	Yellow	Yellow	Yellow
Sycamore Island	Yellow	Red	Red	Yellow	Yellow	Red
Lock 7	Green	Red	Red	Yellow	Yellow	Green
Lock 8	Green	Yellow	Red	Yellow	Yellow	Green
Turkey Run Park	Green	Red	Red	Green	Yellow	Green
Lock 10	Green	Yellow	Red	Yellow	Yellow	Yellow
Scotts Run	Green	Red	Red	Green	Yellow	Yellow
Carderock	Green	Red	Red	Green	Yellow	Yellow
Angler's Inn	Yellow	Yellow	Red	Green	Yellow	Yellow
Great Falls	Green	Yellow	Red	Green	Yellow	Red
Riverbend Regional Park	Green	Green	Green	Green	Yellow	Green
Swains Lock	Green	Yellow	Red	Yellow	Yellow	Yellow
Pennyfield Lock	Yellow	Green	Green	Green	Yellow	Yellow
Seneca Breaks	Green	Yellow	Red	Yellow	Yellow	Green
Fraser Preserve/NoVA	Green	Red	Red	Red	Yellow	Green
Algonkian Regional Park	Yellow	Green	Green	Green	Green	Yellow
Sycamore Landing	Yellow	Yellow	Red	Green	Green	Green
Edwards Ferry	Yellow	Green	Green	Yellow	Green	Yellow
Bles, Mills, Goose Creek	Red	Yellow	Red	Green	Green	Green
Red Rocks Wilderness	Yellow	Red	Red	Green	Green	Red
Balls Bluff Battlefield	Yellow	Red	Red	Green	Green	Red
Whites Ferry	Yellow	Green	Green	Green	Green	Yellow
Dickerson	Yellow	Red	Red	Green	Green	Green
Monocacy	Yellow	Green	Green	Green	Yellow	Green
Nolands Ferry	Yellow	Green	Green	Green	Yellow	Yellow
Point of Rocks	Green	Green	Green	Green	Yellow	Green
Lander	Green	Green	Green	Green	Yellow	Green
Brunswick Campground	Yellow	Green	Green	Green	Yellow	Green
Brunswick Launch	Yellow	Green	Green	Green	Yellow	Yellow
Knoxville Falls	Green	Red	Red	Red	Yellow	Green
Harpers Ferry	Green	Yellow	Red	Red	Yellow	Green

General Directions

Before I get into the specifics of how to get to each location, let's put the region into broad focus. Harpers Ferry and Washington DC anchor the northern and southern extremes with Glen Echo, Great Falls, Leesburg and Brunswick speckling the intervening landscape.

On the Virginia side, Great Falls sits adjacent to the American Legion Bridge and Leesburg straddles the middle section of the river near Whites Ferry. Glen Echo is a bump north of the Chain Bridge in Maryland with the town of Potomac spanning the stretch along River Road from the American Legion Bridge up to Seneca Breaks. Point of Rocks is the next major town up river with Brunswick sitting just downstream from Harpers Ferry.

Inside the Beltway, the George Washington Parkway provides rapid access to Turkey Run and points north while the Clara Barton Parkway is the key road on the Maryland side leading to the great fishing between Chain Bridge and the Anglers Inn.

Beyond the Beltway, Rt 7 is the major artery leading to the close-in fishing locations in Virginia with US 15 North providing the gateway from Leesburg to Point of Rocks. From Leesburg, Rt 9 rolls north toward the smaller feeder roads that dribble into Brunswick and Harpers Ferry from the south. In Maryland, you will get to know River Road extremely well as all of the major fishing locations between the American Legion Bridge and the Dickerson Power Plant require travel along its path.

Coming from the North? From Frederick, US 340 drops traffic into the first-rate fishing in the Harpers Ferry area and allows you to take a quick side trip down US 17 into Brunswick. To get to locations farther south on the Maryland side, use I-270 to reach the small roads that probe down to Dickerson, Whites Ferry and Sycamore Landing.

The detailed directions included with each location assume this level of basic knowledge of geography. However, to make it even easier to find these locations, each chapter includes coordinates you can use in Google Maps to zero in and have Google generate specific and detailed directions from your particular location.

Here is a map of the C&O Canal NHP System from the National Park Service that establishes the big picture and notes the significant roads that will be your routes to the access points.

Here is the geography of the northern section of the system:

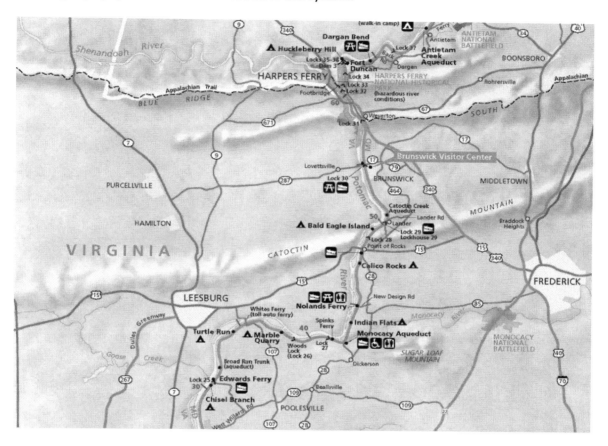

Here is the geography of the southern section of the system:

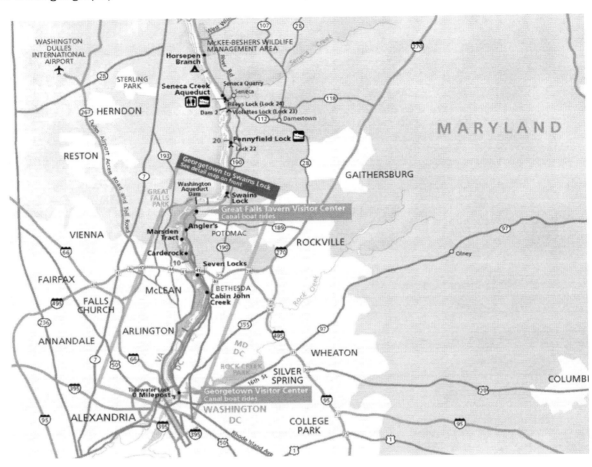

The lower portion of the river between Chain Bridge and Great Falls Park is explicitly addressed in a more detailed map available from the National Park Service.

Here is the upper portion of the segment between Swains Lock and Lock 10:

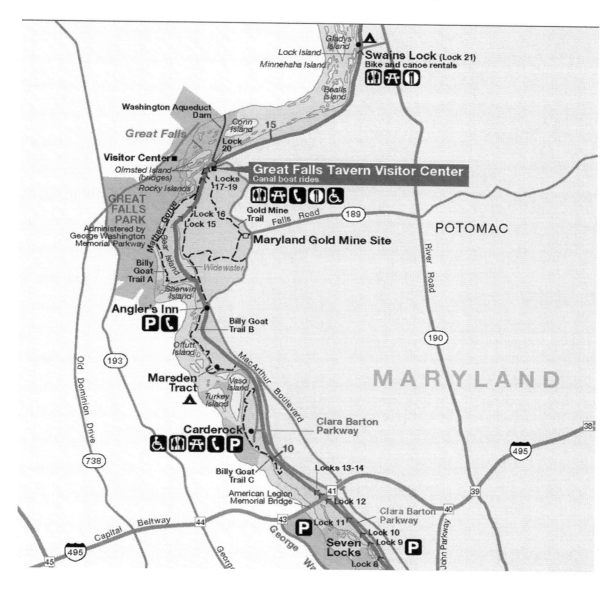

The remainder of the lower segment between Lock 10 and Milepost 0:

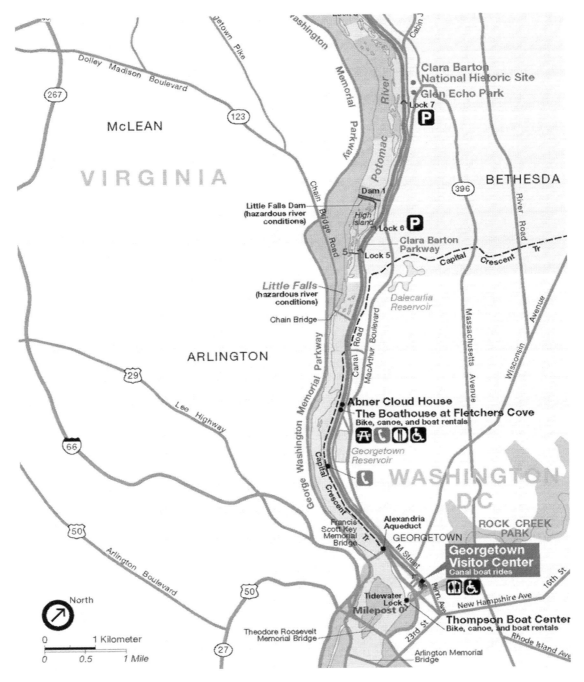

Chain Bridge

Google Map Coordinates: 38.932361,-77.11315

Summary Rating

Pressure	Yellow	Canoe/Kayak Launch	Red
Physical Fitness	Red	Trailer Boat Launch	Red
Wading	Red	Parking	Green
Shore Fishing	Green	Regulations	Yellow
Spin Fishing	Green	Fly Fishing	Yellow
Scenery	Green	Overall	Yellow

Special Regulations

There are no special fishing regulations in effect here. However, for approximately a half mile upstream of the Chain Bridge, the river is controlled by the District.

As you drive down the Clara Barton Parkway, the big, green sign marking the border looms large immediately north of the parking area at the bridge. Remember that location because south of that spot you need a District license; above that point either a Maryland or Virginia license will work. If you have a GPS, the coordinates of the boundary are approximately 38.934727,-77.119324.

Getting to the Stream

North: From I-495, take either the Cabin John or Clara Barton Parkway south. Proceed south for 3.5 miles. The parking area (38.932361,-77.11315) is on the right immediately prior to reaching the Chain Bridge.

South: From I-395, take exit 10C towards the George Washington Memorial Parkway. Follow it for approximately 7 miles to the SR 123 S/Chain Bridge exit. Leave at that exit and follow it to the dead end on Chain Bridge Road. Turn left to go across the bridge, left again at the light and the parking area is on the left.

There is plenty of parking, but no direct access to the canal. You must walk down to the bridge and use the pedestrian overpass to cross the canal to reach the towpath.

If the main parking area is full, there is an alternate parking area on the western side of the Chain Bridge. It includes a small amount of parking on the shoulder with a few additional slots underneath the bridge supporting the George Washington Memorial Parkway.

Caution: The water is deep and fast here. Exercise extra care if you fish this section.

Environment and Fish

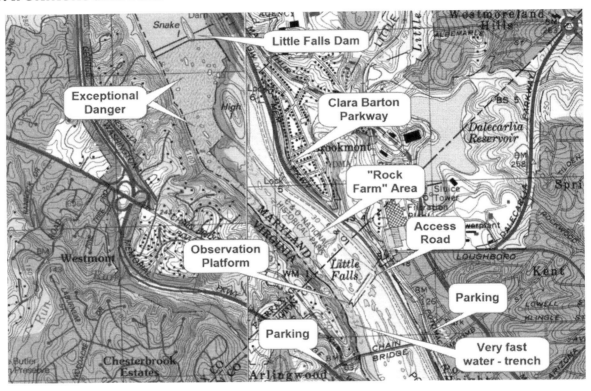

I have not fished here since it is not worth it to me to buy a District fishing license for this single spot. I have done an extensive reconnaissance of this area, walked the shoreline and conclude that it looks good and should be productive. If you invest in a District license, you can put it to excellent use here.

As a transitional comment that links the start point at the Chain Bridge with the water downstream, one of the fact checkers with the New Horizon Bass Anglers club who reviewed the book prior to publication pointed out that the area on the east side of the river for about a mile south of the bridge has pretty good fishing. He told me that the river runs slower in that section with good rock structure and even a few places to wade. Just like other areas inside the Beltway, he pointed out that it's odd to hear the traffic rumbling on the other side of the trees or the cliffs while in the middle of good smallmouth fishing. You may have to do some bushwhacking to move from the towpath to the river as there are a limited number of trails. The final caveat is the same as I make as we move upstream. Access to the river proper is dependent on water levels and that is complicated by the tidal influence that reaches up to this area. You can purchase your district license directly from the fisheries and wildlife Department at ddoe.dc.gov or at the Fletcher's boathouse. But, enough about that -- let's jump into the river at the Chain Bridge and move north.

The area around the Chain Bridge is surprisingly scenic for being located in the heart of the metropolitan area. This is deep water. The river tightens as it approaches the bridge and the full force of the water is channeled into a narrow trench. Be sure you put enough weight on your lure to get it down deep enough in the fast moving water column to be interesting to the fish.

As you move north towards Maryland, the river remains tight, fast and violent. That said, there are loads of interesting looking places you can fish from the bank. You should target the current breaks and the seams created by the churn of fast water next to the calmer pools.

Once on the towpath, walk north to the intersection of the towpath with a wide, overgrown, asphalt/concrete road at approximately 38.93511,-77.11581. Turn left on the old road and follow it to the observation platform overlooking the river. You can fish up or downstream along the shore. Approximately 900 feet upstream from the platform, the unmarked border between the District and Maryland creates a transition where the river broadens into the rock farm. At high water, the river fills some shallow lakes between the main stem of the river and the towpath. They are not worth fishing since they become stagnant when the water recedes.

You will feel like a gladiator walking into the arena as you walk down the improved road from the towpath.

The road bed is smooth and solid -- no mud -- but the rock walls close in on both sides.

Once you start down the path, your only exit is at the observation platform at the end where you gain access to the river.

This is the view downstream from the observation platform. The river is fishable from the shore.

Caution! Note the turbulence in the water as it careens downstream and exercise caution. Wear a PFD when fishing from the shore. Two anglers drowned in early 2009 when they slipped into the water.

The Little Falls gage height was 3.29 ft on the day this picture was taken.

Upstream, the river narrows and becomes extremely deep.

Use a full sink tip if fly fishing or weight your lure if using spin gear.

Bottom Line

Given the fast-moving water in this section, you must not wade. One false step on the slick river bottom and you could find yourself careening downstream in big trouble. In addition, this is a very popular stretch given the class IV-V rapids that exist downstream from Little Falls and you should expect to encounter kayakers on sunny days. If you fish this stretch, come when the water level is low.

Lock 6

Google Map Coordinates: 38.94384,-77.12346

Summary Rating

Pressure	Yellow	Canoe/Kayak Launch	Red
Physical Fitness	Red	Trailer Boat Launch	Red
Wading	Red	Parking	Yellow
Shore Fishing	Green	Regulations	Yellow
Spin Fishing	Green	Fly Fishing	Yellow
Scenery	Yellow	Overall	Yellow

Special Regulations

Be alert for the boundary with the District towards the southern end of the Lock 6 section. It's easy to find since the Little Falls Branch cuts across the towpath just north of the boundary. As long as you stay on the northern side, either a Maryland or Virginia license will keep you legal.

For licensing, this area is considered part of the Tidal Potomac. As such, you need a tidal license (different from a normal freshwater license) to fish anywhere between Chain Bridge and the Little Falls Dam.

Finally, by Maryland law, anglers must wear a US Coast Guard approved personal flotation device (PFD) while fishing in the river in the area below the Little Falls Dam to the border with the District.

Getting to the Stream

North: From I-495, take either the Cabin John or Clara Barton Parkway south. The Cabin John joins the Clara Barton Parkway. From that junction, continue south for just over 2.4 miles. The parking area (38.94384,-77.12346) is on the right.

South: The parking area at Lock 6 is not accessible from the south. If you travel from the south, follow the George Washington Parkway to I-495 and take the exit towards Maryland. Once over the bridge, take the Clara Barton exit towards Glen Echo (exit 41) and follow the Clara Barton Parkway south as described above.

The parking area at Lock 6 is well marked and has a decent amount of parking. It can get very busy on the weekends, so get here early.

If you drive farther south past the Lock 6 parking lot, you might get excited when you see what appears to be a parking area at Lock 5 (38.939934,-77.121685). You will probably see other people parked here, but this is not a legal parking area and that fact is noted with small "no parking" signs at both ends of the open area. Granted, parking at Lock 5 puts you in the middle of the "rock farm" within an easy walk of the best fishing in this section, but it's better to get some extra exercise than a ticket. Besides, you could knock your front end out of alignment bumping over the curb at high speed.

Once parked, head to the northern side of the lot and follow the trail past the Lock House to the bridge across the canal.

This is the open area at Lock 5 with two cars waiting for their ticket. It's deceptive because it looks like a parking lot.

The "no parking" signs are at both ends of the open area. They are easy to miss because the signs are the ones you would expect to see on the street - the small kind on a tall pole that says "no parking" with an arrow pointing to the illegal section.

Environment and Fish

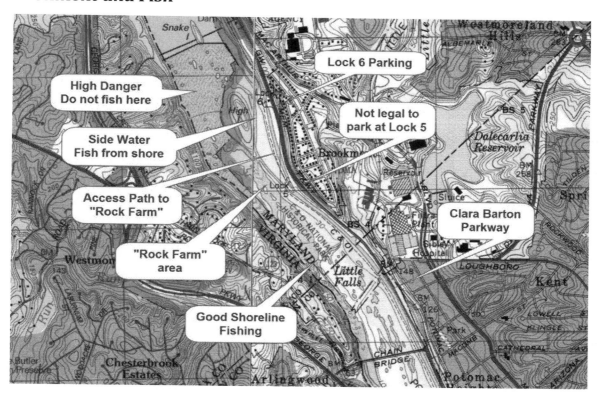

There are two distinct areas near Lock 6 that deserve your attention. The first is what I call the "side water", followed by the "rock farm" another quarter-mile south. Before I discuss those, I must strongly caution you against fishing upstream into the area directly below the Little Falls Dam. It is one of the most dangerous areas on the Potomac. The rapids are large and violent; with some reaching class IV or V status. Instead, work downstream from the parking lot to lower your risk.

Side Water

Your first choice after crossing the canal will be to decide how far you want to walk to fish. You can begin your day right here if you want to fish the side water that spins around the eastern chute from the Little Falls Dam. To reach it, follow the small path that intersects the towpath near the bridge. It will take you directly to the shoreline.

After taking a curious look at the depth markers and absorbing how deep and violent this river can become during the high water period in the spring, start fishing downstream on the shoreline. You need to use spin gear because the shoreline is tight and close. There is no room for an easy backcast using fly gear. In addition, since the water is deep - far too deep to wade - spin gear provides better lure and weight options.

That said the side water is fairly uninteresting. If you did not realize that you were next to the Potomac, it would be easy to conclude you were on the shoreline of a calm lake. At normal flows, the current is imperceptible until you get to the southern section where the water breaks over a small dam to rejoin the river.

This is the view upstream from where the small path joins the side water.

Note the depth markers suspended above the water - take pause and consider how serious of a mistake it would be fish here during high water.

Rock Farm

I recommend that you ignore the side water and walk directly downstream to find the rock farm. A short quarter-mile walk south on the towpath puts you at the intersection (38.94178,-77.12294) of a wide "road" that leads to the west towards the river. If you were to follow the small, tight shoreline trail that parallels the side water, you would eventually reach the same place with a lot more effort. There is no need to bushwhack when you can move swiftly down the towpath on foot or on a bike to get the same place.

The road ends at an old structure supporting a footbridge across the top that is the gateway to the shoreline. After a little bit of bushwhacking down a gentle slope, the great vista of the river unfolds. Not great in terms of the distance you can see, but great in terms of the smallmouth friendly structure.

As you scan your surroundings, you see rocks poking out of the water; dotting the surface in all directions. Many of these feature thin rock fingers stretching from the shore into the heart of the river. Remember that Maryland law requires you to wear a PFD.

Looking upstream from vicinity of 38.940512,-77.123728.

This is the upper boundary of the rock farm. There are plenty of rock ridges stretching into the river that provide lateral movement.

The rocks continue upstream all the way around the island in the distance.

Downstream from this point, the river broadens out to form a "lake" that collects on the east side of the river; pushing against the catcher's mitt created by the slightly higher ground at the left of this picture.

If you look at the satellite view on Google Maps, you will get a good perspective of the "catch basin."

The main channel is to the west.

The rock farm continues south along the Maryland shoreline.

The lower the water is, the easier it becomes to move on the rock ridges to get closer to the main channel. Caution -- do not even think about wading in the main channel!

The Little Falls gage height was 3.29 ft on the day this picture was taken

This is the southern end of the catch basin. The high ground is at the left of the picture.

Spring flooding covers the entire area and creates small, stagnant "ponds" between the river and the towpath.

Little Falls Branch

As you walk south on the towpath to reach the southern end of Lock 6, be alert for the stream that cuts across the canal and dribbles towards the river. The junction of the stream and the towpath is at 38.93707,-77.11806. Assuming you do not have a District fishing license, you need to stay on the northern side of the stream.

There are two faint paths, one on either side, that lead to the river. Take the northern path. The closer you get to the river, the fainter the path becomes until it eventually disappears. At that point, step over fallen trees and climb over moderate sized rocks to reach the junction. It's worth the walk, because when you get there, you will be at the southern end of the rock farm.

The water begins to channel tightly as it approaches Chain Bridge. Until you move farther upstream, safety restricts fishing to the shoreline since the water is deep and fast.

That said this is a decent spot as long as you can get your lure deep. Fly anglers must deploy a full sinking line and spin fisherman can use anything in their arsenal.

Looking upstream from the junction of the Little Falls Branch.

Good rock ledges extend into the river.

Note the rough water to the left of the picture.

The Little Falls gage height was 3.29 feet on the day this picture was taken.

The view downstream towards the Chain Bridge shows the increasing danger of the river as it compresses to enter the narrow channel leading up to the bridge.

Bottom line

If you have a tidal license, there is decent fishing between the junction of the Little Falls Branch and the start of the rough water at the base of the dam. I strongly recommend that you stay at least a half mile downstream of the dam and even then, exercise extraordinary caution. This entire section is dangerous given the way the water channels into tight, fast chutes that are a joy for kayakers but could spell death for anglers.

Sycamore Island

Google Map Coordinates: 38.95808,-77.13153

Summary Rating

Pressure	Green	Canoe/Kayak Launch	Red
Physical Fitness	Red	Trailer Boat Launch	Red
Wading	Red	Parking	Yellow
Shore Fishing	Red	Regulations	Yellow
Spin Fishing	Green	Fly Fishing	Red
Scenery	Yellow	Overall	Red

Special Regulations

None.

Getting to the Stream

North: From I-495, take either the Cabin John or Clara Barton Parkway south. The Cabin John joins the Clara Barton Parkway. From that junction, continue south for just over 1.4 miles. The parking area (38.95808,-77.13153) is on the right.

South: From I-395, take exit 10C towards the George Washington Memorial Parkway. Follow it for approximately 7 miles to the SR 123 S/Chain Bridge exit. Leave at that exit and follow it to the dead end on Chain Bridge Road. Turn left to go across the bridge, left again at the light. Follow Chain Bridge Road north for approximately 2.2 miles. The parking area is on the left.

There is a pedestrian ramp across the parkway at the north end of the parking lot. The path to the river starts at the base of the ramp.

As you walk towards the pedestrian ramp from the parking area, you may be tempted to walk down this rough trail that leads directly to the suspension bridge visible through the trees.

Don't bother, if you continue to the pedestrian walkway, a moderate pitched, wide path leads to the same place without the risk of a bad fall.

Environment and Fish

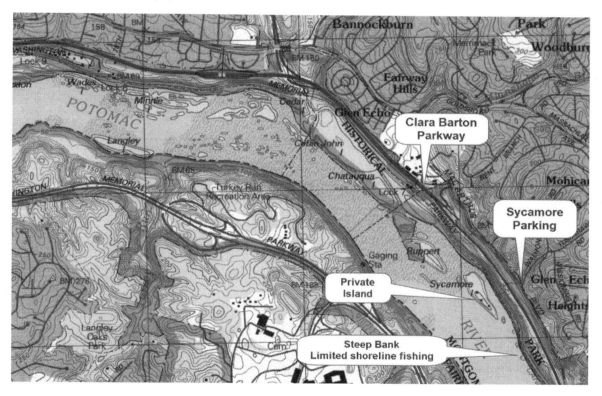

I include this location not because it is good, but because it is horrible. A key reason to report the bad spots is to keep you from wasting a sunny afternoon and a long drive only to be disappointed upon arrival.

After walking down the steep hill, cross the suspension bridge to reach the towpath. Immediately upstream of the suspension bridge is the hand-operated ferry that members of the Sycamore Island Club use to get out onto their private island. You can check out the small ferry, but don't do anything with it. Instead, look up and downriver and assess the boring panorama.

The banks are precipitous and there is no room to walk along the shoreline next to the water without clinging desperately onto the thick vegetation that carpets the bank. The water is deep, really deep. Immediately downstream of this location, the Little Falls Dam backs up the river for a considerable distance; creating the broad, deep "lake" that is only accessible using a boat. Even boaters need to be careful and obey the warning buoys stretched across the river just upstream of the head of the dam.

If you are fixated on fishing here, there are a few places where you can slide down the steep bank to stand in a single location and throw a lure into the deep, dark water. Don't bring your fly fishing gear since there is no room for a backcast.

This is the view up river between the towpath and Sycamore Island at 38.958057,-77.132558.

The small cable used to control the private ferry runs across the top of the picture.

The Little Falls gage height was 3.29 ft on the day this picture was taken.

This is the view towards the Little Falls Dam from that same location.

Immediately beyond the southern tip of Sycamore Island, Potomac turns into "big" water with no visible surface structure as a result of the backup of water from the Little Falls Dam.

Boaters should not go any closer to the dam than the string of buoys that provide an obvious warning of the danger to come.

There are large, white signs on either side of the river that literally scream at boaters to get to the shore and not proceed any farther downstream.

Taken from 38.95465,-77.13048.

This is the suspension bridge that links the towpath with the parking area.

Late in the season, scum builds up on the water in the canal and there is a distinct odor that can assault sensitive nostrils if you're here on the wrong day.

Bottom line

This is not a scenic spot and you should avoid this place if you want to have a good day of fishing. Access is limited, the water is big, and it just not right unless you have a boat. Even when you use a boat, fishing puts you dangerously close to the dam.

Lock 7

Google Map Coordinates: 38.964297,-77.138207

Summary Rating

Pressure	Yellow	Canoe/Kayak Launch	Red
Physical Fitness	Yellow	Trailer Boat Launch	Red
Wading	Yellow	Parking	Yellow
Shore Fishing	Green	Regulations	Yellow
Spin Fishing	Yellow	Fly Fishing	Green
Scenery	Green	Overall	Yellow

Special Regulations

None.

Getting to the Stream

North: From I-495 , take either the Cabin John or Clara Barton Parkway south. The Cabin John joins the Clara Barton Parkway. From that junction, continue south for just over 0.8 miles. The parking area (38.964297,-77.138207) is on the right.

South: The parking area at Lock 7 is not accessible from the south. If you travel from the south, follow the George Washington Parkway to where it intersects I-495 and take the exit towards Maryland. From I-495, use the Clara Barton exit towards Glen Echo (exit 41) and follow the Clara Barton Parkway south as described above.

Parking is limited on weekends because this is a popular destination for the hiking and biking crowds. If you're going to fish, get here early enough to get a spot. Once you park, walk to the north end of the parking area and follow the trail down the hill on the left side of the small picnic table to walk past the Lock House and cross the canal.

This is the access trail down to the canal.

It goes down a small hill and then turns sharply left across the canal to the towpath.

Environment and Fish

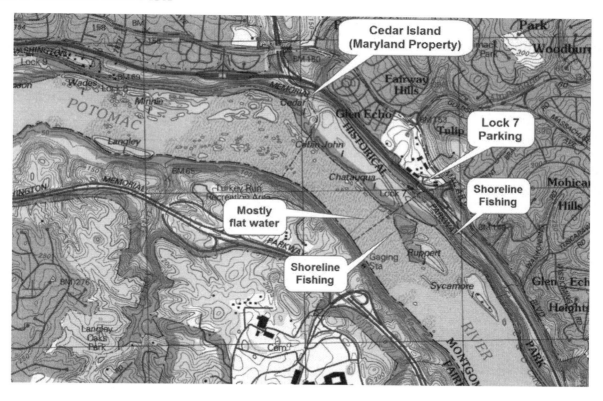

Starting from the south, the first access point is 0.4 miles from the parking area where a well-defined trail leads to the river (38.96207,-77.13643). Unfortunately, it is a wasted walk for waders. When you break through the scraggly bush on the riverbank, the water is uniformly deep. While there is a decent amount of current stirring the water, this is the northern headwater of the lake backed up by the Little Falls Dam.

From the shore, you can look at Ruppert Island and see the main body of the river with the hint of rocky structure beyond. This is not the place to attempt a crossing. If you enjoy fishing from the shore, this is a good spot. The shoreline is wide enough to move easily in either direction. The trees are thick and anxious to snag your backcast, so use spin gear.

Back at the parking area, you find the best and quickest access to the river. Follow the obvious trail on the other side of the bridge to the river's edge. This puts you at a shallow, narrow chute between Chatauqua and Ruppert Islands (38.96333, -77.13966). At low water, you can walk across to Ruppert Island to gain access to the random rock ridges that stretch into the river on its western shore.

There are well defined rock ridges extending perpendicular to the shore that provide easy access to the center of the river. However, as I will discuss in the Harpers Ferry area, these are "in and out" ridges. In the case of Lock 7, they hang just below the surface with only a hint of definition poking above the water level. The water is unwadeable on either side; your movement is restricted to the sporadically submerged ridgeline. If you prefer to fish from the shore, this is a good spot since the shoreline is open with easy travel through the rocks that border a gentle bank. Even fly anglers can fish from the shore on Ruppert Island if they pick their location carefully.

One word of caution that applies to the entire section from the Chain Bridge up to Lock 10 is that you should mark your entry point carefully. Once you are out in the river, the shoreline looks the same. Failure to do so will result in some fairly tough bushwhacking to get back to the towpath. The good news is that it is impossible to get lost since the towpath follows the river; the challenge will be to get back to the towpath. In the case of Lock 7, if you enter at the parking area, you will probably go into the river at the gap between the two islands. Take a look at that spot once you get beyond the fallen tree that straddles the gap and make a mental note.

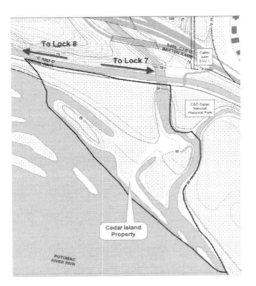

Another option to gain access to the river is to walk 0.6 miles up the towpath to the Maryland owned Cedar Island property. It overlaps the towpath in the vicinity of 38.96986, -77.14719.

From there, you can walk down to the river in the vicinity of Cabin John Island and work the many faster runs and chutes that exist in this area at lower water levels. You can reach the same location by walking 0.8 miles from Lock 8.

This is the view downstream from the shoreline at the end of the path that starts at 38.96207,-77.13643.

The overhanging vegetation makes it impossible to use fly gear in this location.

However, it is fishable with spin gear and the shoreline is accessible.

This is the view upstream from that same location.

The main channel of the river is beyond Ruppert Island.

At low water, you can walk out to the island from near the Lock House and then fish down the shoreline.

The trail from the Lock House leads to the tip of the string of islands that border of the main channel of the river.

While there is a small amount of water present in this picture, at low water you can walk across to the island without wading.

This picture was taken looking upstream from where the trail joins the river.

Straight out from the trailhead, there is more water and good structure in front of you. This is the shallow chute where water spills between the two islands. At low water this can dry up or only be inches deep.

If you do not want to wade, the best way to get to the islands is to walk upstream to 38.96587,-77.14104 where the side channel dries up. From there, you can follow the shoreline of Chatauqua Island down to Ruppert.

To the left from the trailhead, the river broadens out and becomes deeper.

You have to wade across this shallow channel to get to the island.

The Little Falls gage height was 3.29 ft on the day this picture was taken – higher than I prefer.

The view looking downriver from the main channel with Ruppert Island on the left.

The shoreline sports plenty of structure as well as an accessible bank.

The Point of Rocks gage read 1.37 ft when this picture was taken while the Little Falls gage was at 2.72 - perfect conditions.

Rocks and fallen trees mark deeper structure. Each of these shelters plenty of sunfish and smallmouth bass.

The wide view of the shoreline shows a long, rocky front.

It's easy to fish down the shoreline; you can use the rocks to reach a little farther out into the river in some spots.

Bottom Line

Lock 7 is a good fishing destination at the right water level. You have a wide variety of choices depending on whether you want to fish from the shore or wade. Both fly and spin anglers will have a good day here because, regardless of what type of equipment you use, you can reach good water.

Lock 8

Google Map Coordinates: 38.97160,-77.16058

Summary Rating

Pressure	Yellow	Canoe/Kayak Launch	Yellow
Physical Fitness	Yellow	Trailer Boat Launch	Red
Wading	Green	Parking	Yellow
Shore Fishing	Green	Regulations	Yellow
Spin Fishing	Yellow	Fly Fishing	Green
Scenery	Green	Overall	Green

Special Regulations

None.

Getting to the Stream

North: From I-495, take either the Cabin John or Clara Barton Parkway south. The Cabin John joins the Clara Barton Parkway. From that junction, continue a short distance south past the parking for Lock 10 to the clearly marked turnout for Lock 8 (38.97160,-77.16058) on the right.

South: The parking area at Lock 8 is not accessible from the south. If you travel from the south, follow the George Washington Parkway to where it intersects I-495 and take the exit towards Maryland. From I-495, turn at the Clara Barton exit towards Glen Echo (exit 41) and follow the Clara Barton Parkway south as described above.

Use the turnout for Lock 10 as the landmark warning of the upcoming turn into Lock 8. Walk to the north end of the parking lot and follow the trail down a moderate hill to the canal. The Lock House will be on the left and the bridge across the canal is next to it.

Some older books mention a boat ramp at Lock 8. At best, it's a spot at the end of a scraggly trail where you can dump a kayak into the river.

The quickest and easiest approach to the river is on the wide path next to the Lock House.

Environment and Fish

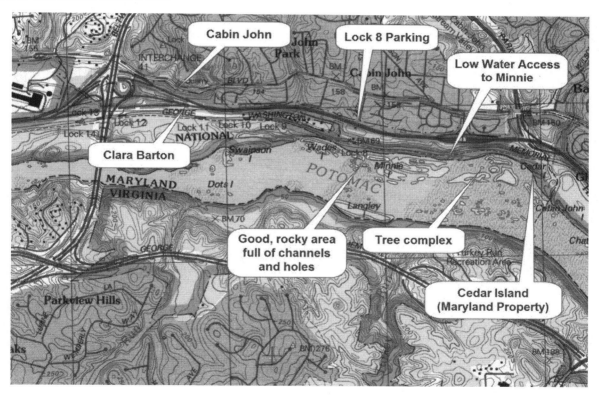

You have several options at Lock 8. Starting from below the Lock, if you walk 0.6 miles south on the towpath, the first access point will pop up on the right (38.97029,-77.15300). Between the Lock House and this point, the boundary between the towpath and the river is a stark, bright line defined by a steep drop. The towpath breaks left at the entry point, moving away from the river, with a gentle slope extending to the river from the turn. Once there, assuming the water is low enough, you can walk out onto the series of small islands that guard the river bank from the main thrust of the river.

Cedar Island is another 0.25 miles down the towpath and is in the heart of the island complex that offers some great fishing at normal water levels. The water runs quick and strong between the numerous small islands that dot this corner of the river.

The small islands offer good purchase for spin fishing. Unless you can move away from the islands on a rock ridge, your ability to fly fish will be limited as a result of the brush that piles up to the edge of the shore on each of these islands.

The towpath runs right next to the river and the bank is steep. At 38.97029,-77.15300, you can get down to the river without having to fall off a cliff.

This picture was taken looking upstream and you can see the small dribble of water that separates the main river from the towpath.

When the water is low during the summer, you can cross here without wading.

Looking downstream towards Cedar island from the same point, scattered islands covered with trees extend to the horizon

The water is usually shallow and runs across a rocky bottom.

Another way to get out onto the islands is by entering from Cedar Island.

This is another view out into the main section of the river and, if you look closely, you can see the rocks on the bottom showing through the thin layer of water that covers them.

The Point of Rocks gage read 1.75 ft when this picture was taken while the Little Falls gage was 3.29 ft.

The next access point is directly across from the Lock House. There is a wide, obvious path that leads to the river.

This location offers the best opportunity to work your way down the shoreline and out onto the rocky ridges without wading. At the low point in the summer, you can move onto some of the barrier islands and, from there, onto the rock ridges.

There is a good view of the American Legion Bridge in the distance. As the trucks lumber across that major artery, it's hard to comprehend you are standing in one of the East Coast's best smallmouth rivers. This particular slice of heaven is speckled with rocks, ridges and ledges that all shelter cuts with runs ending in deeper pools; all are infested with bass. Once fly anglers get out onto the rock ridges, they will have a hard time keeping the sunfish off their fly. This is the perfect place to use small poppers flipped up against the rocks that border the deep spots.

Spin fishers will have a rough day as a result of the ragged structure that litters the bottom of the river. Any presentation that is not weedless runs the risk of hanging up on one of the cracks in the many ledges that stretch across the river. Stick to grubs or 4 to 6 inch worms rigged weedless and bounce them along the bottom.

The "barrier islands" provide a good view upstream towards the American Legion bridge.

There is plenty of room to move around the river or on the shoreline.

The Point of Rocks gage was 1.62 ft when this picture was taken. The Little Falls gage was 2.88 ft.

The view downstream along the shoreline is just as encouraging.

There are plenty of ridges that stretch into the river.

The farther you can get away from the shoreline, the more likely it is you will catch larger bass except when they huddle in the shade during the heat of the summer.

Downstream along the shore, the water opens up with fewer rock structures in evidence. Many of the ridges downstream run just under the surface of the water.

At the right time of year, you can move a decent distance into the river on the ridges.

The Point of Rocks gage read 1.62 ft when this picture was taken while the Little Falls gage was 2.88 ft.

Bottom line

You have unlimited wading opportunities. In addition, shore fishers can leverage the relatively open shoreline around Wades and Minnie Islands. The numerous rock ledges and other structure that exists make this an ideal destination for a full day of fishing.

Turkey Run Park

Google Map Coordinates: 38.964464,-77.153184

Summary Rating

Pressure	Red	Canoe/Kayak Launch	Red
Physical Fitness	Red	Trailer Boat Launch	Red
Wading	Green	Parking	Green
Shore Fishing	Yellow	Regulations	Yellow
Spin Fishing	Yellow	Fly Fishing	Green
Scenery	Green	Overall	Green

Special Regulations

Bikes are not allowed on the trails in the Park.

Getting to the Stream

Get onto the George Washington Parkway. The exit for Turkey Run Park is plainly marked regardless of whether you're coming from the north or the south. The exit is at the northern end of the George Washington Parkway, so be patient if you're coming from the south. The exit leads directly to the Park. Take the first turn to go to both of the parking areas; first passing by the upper parking lot (38.964464,-77.153184) and ending at the lower parking lot at the bottom of the hill (38.963004,-77.148523).

The 700 acre Turkey Run Park is located upon a bluff overlooking the Potomac River. It is a harder hike down to the shoreline from the upper parking lot than from the lower as a result of the steep pitch of the hill. The Potomac Heritage Trail runs through the park.

Environment and Fish

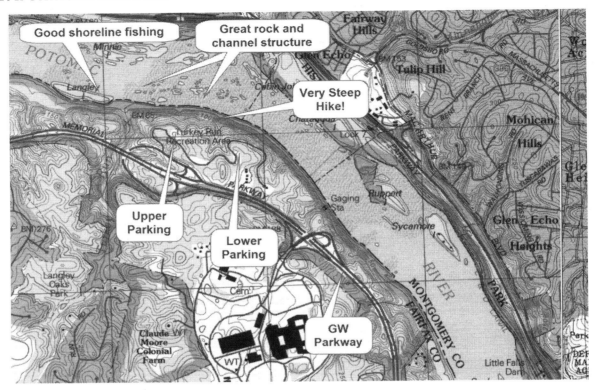

The trailhead at the upper parking lot is near the northeast corner. Walk by the kiosk to start down the steep pitch on a narrow, well maintained trail to reach the river. There are plenty of switchbacks to make the trek a little easier on the half mile walk, but nothing can hide the fact that the trail drops a little over 200 vertical feet in a short distance.

As a result of the current break provided by Langley Island (38.96651, -77.15910), the water in the immediate vicinity of Turkey Run Park is calmer than the rest of the river. However, once you move farther into the main stream of the river, the current shows its muscle and demands caution as you move from place to place. The shoreline is pleasant in the vicinity of Langley Island; wide and accommodating. Unfortunately for shoreline fishers, the water remains relatively shallow near the banks with only a few deep cuts within easy casting distance.

For those who wade, plenty of rock ridges facilitate movement away from the shoreline and are most noticeably present during periods of low water. In fact, this is one of the rockier areas in this part of the Potomac. The broken structure is one of the great joys that fly anglers can take advantage of. Many of the rocks huddle next to deeper holes and provide easy targets for gently landed poppers or larger terrestrial patterns that produce explosive reactions from the waiting smallmouth. The current is fast enough to allow the effective deployment of streamers and other patterns that need a bit of a push from the water column to provide life and action.

Spin fishers will be frustrated using anything except weedless presentations. Texas rigged grubs and other types of plastics are good choices given the snag prone bottom. I recommend against using spinners or crank baits except where you can visually confirm the hole is deep enough to prevent hangups. The bottom is full of rocks and jagged cracks whose only purpose on this earth is to snag your lure.

There is another trail that leads to the river from the lower parking lot. However, the only information kiosk is at the upper parking lot. You should stop there to review the maps and information posted since it will orient you on the different river access options and trails.

Turkey Run Park is directly across from Lock 8.

The view upstream to the American Legion Bridge is warmly satisfying as you fish and contemplate the thousands of other less fortunate souls commuting to work.

Langley Island is at the top left of this picture and provides a glimpse of the open spaces on the shoreline that make for easy movement. It's not unusual to see hikers walking along the shoreline enjoying the scenery.

At summer pool, there are more rocks than water.

At the base of the hill where the trail joins the shoreline, the rock ridges give anglers plenty of different options to move out into the river.

The Point of Rocks gage read 1.08 ft and the Little Falls gage was 2.59 ft when this picture was taken.

This is the view towards Lock 8.

Unless you look upstream at the American Legion Bridge, it is easy to believe that you are in the middle of the wilderness even though you are only a few miles from the heart of the District.

With the exception of a few random houses, there is no urban sprawl to disrupt your view.

The view downstream shows rock ridges that facilitate movement towards the center of the river.

Even at low water, there are many good runs and deeper pools clustered close to the shore.

Fly anglers will have a field day in this area.

Bottom line

Turkey Run is a good fishing destination. It's well maintained with a minimum of litter. In fact, it's rare to find the scattered bait containers that seem to be ubiquitous at other locations. The gentle shoreline near Langley Island facilitates movement for those who prefer not to use the rock ridges to access the river. There are many areas along the shoreline that are wide enough to support a fly angler's backcast without having to get into the water.

It's amazing that such a scenic spot can exist inside the Beltway. For those who work along the northern beltway and face a tough commute home, I recommend throwing a rod into your trunk and spend an hour or two fishing instead of sitting in traffic.

If you do that, remember that Turkey Run Park, like all of the gated parks, will close at sunset. Be sure you to leave before the staff locks the gate.

Lock 10

Google Map Coordinates: 38.97263,-77.16899

Summary Rating

Pressure	Yellow	Canoe/Kayak Launch	Yellow
Physical Fitness	Yellow	Trailer Boat Launch	Red
Wading	Red	Parking	Yellow
Shore Fishing	Green	Regulations	Yellow
Spin Fishing	Green	Fly Fishing	Green
Scenery	Green	Overall	Yellow

Special Regulations

None.

Getting to the Stream

North: From the I-495 Beltway, take either the Cabin John or Clara Barton Parkway south. The Cabin John joins the Clara Barton Parkway. At that junction, swing right to enter the parking lot at 38.97263,-77.16899. You will not have much room to execute the maneuver and need to watch for fast-moving traffic approaching from the right.

South: The parking area at Lock 10 is not accessible from the south. Approaching from the south, follow the George Washington Parkway to where it intersects I-495 and take the exit towards Maryland. From I-495, turn at the Clara Barton exit towards Glen Echo (exit 41) and follow the Clara Barton Parkway south as described above

The parking area at Lock 10 is fairly large, but fills up quickly on weekends.

Access to the towpath is obvious and easy with no steep hills to negotiate.

The best places to reach the river are a short walk up or downstream.

Environment and Fish

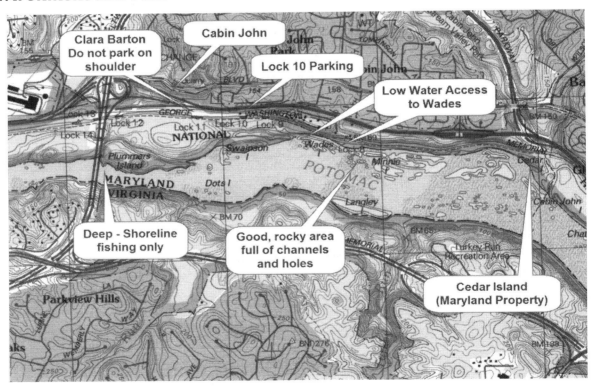

Lock 10 is a good place to fish with either spin or fly gear. In general, the shoreline is easy to navigate, accessible and provides opportunities to move out on ledges to keep your backcast with out of the trees. The main terrain feature is a large, long and narrow island called Swainson Island. While it is covered with trees and vegetation, it's not thick to the point of being impenetrable and does not create a significant obstacle preventing you from reaching the river.

You have three basic choices, two are good and one is marginal:

- You can walk downstream a quarter-mile to great-looking water (good)
- You can start fishing near the parking lot (marginal)
- You can walk up to the I-495 bridge near Lock 12 (good)

This is a true angler's dilemma! So much water, so little time.

Lower Area

A quick quarter-mile walk on the towpath puts you at the southern end of Swainson Island. Instead of bushwhacking through the thick vegetation searching for a place to cross over to the island, walk down to 38.97171,-77.16443 where it's easy to cross the muddy flats created when the backwater dries up at the height of summer. The towpath is next to the river and a quick slide down a gentle bank provides direct access to the river via Wades Island. You can fish up or downstream from here -- it's all good since you are in the middle of a rocky area with plenty of ridges surrounding deeper holes.

This is the view of the area that becomes a muddy flat at low water in the summer and allows easy access to the ridge of islands that extend downstream from Lock 10.

From these islands, it's easy to move out into the rock ridges that stretch towards Virginia.

Looking straight out from 38.97171,-77.16443, the main channel is visible beyond Wades Island in the foreground of the picture.

There is a plethora of good rocks to fish in this area.

The Point of Rocks gage was at 1.75 ft and the Little Falls gage as at 3.29 ft when this picture was taken.

You can work out on the various rock ridges in this section and pepper the water for 360°.

Lock 10 is close to the American Legion Bridge. This is a great place to come for afternoon fishing while you wait for the traffic to die down.

At the height of summer, daylight lingers and the bass are active -- a perfect combination for a great end to a tough workday

This is the view to the southwest towards the eastern tip of Swainson Island (38.97171,-77.16443).

The area immediately downstream of Swainson Island forms a large, shallow backwater lake. Wades Island is to the immediate left of this picture.

The Point of Rocks gage was at 1.51 ft when this picture was taken.

Looking to the left down the southern shoreline of Wades Island, there are numerous rock ridges that provide easy access to the river.

The best place to fish is where the water is moving. Sunfish guard the still pools, but the bass prefer moving water. So, follow the current through the breaks between the rocks and fish the seams.

This picture looks across the river towards Virginia and provides a good view of the Virginia shoreline 0.5 miles upstream of Turkey Run Park.

This is a wider view looking downstream from Wades Island. The river is dotted with good structure comprised of rocky outcroppings connected by underwater ledges.

There are some deep holes here so you should wear a PFD and be careful.

Middle – Across the Bridge

Take the trail that joins the towpath near the bridge. Your walk ends at the intersection of several stretches of backwater that retain depth even in the summer. To get to the river, the best approach is to follow the channel to your left until you find a place to cross. Swainson Island has steep sides that require crawling hand over foot up an aggressive pitch if you pick the wrong place. Once on the other side, the broad sweep of the river lies to the front; populated with plenty of rocks peeking up above the surface protected by deep holes and a swirling current.

But, the farther south you walk, the closer you get to the lower area already discussed. It's much easier to walk the quarter-mile to the lower access point on the towpath than beat your way along the backwater behind Swainson Island. However, there are plenty of people who are content to perch on the edge of the backwater or walk over to Swainson Island to fish the deep water on the other side.

When you reach the river from the trail near the bridge across the towpath, this is what you will see at 38.97142, -77.16851.

This is the side channel on the near side of Swainson island. The main river is on the other side of the stand of trees in the distance.

There are a lot of people who fish from the shore in this location.

The backwater area is to the left and remains deep and stagnant until it dries in the summer heat.

Instead of working down the shoreline to the left to dodge around the small extension of the island on the right, stick to the towpath and walk directly to the lower area.

Lock 12 / I-495 Bridge

A good option for deep water is to walk 0.6 miles west on the towpath to reach Lock 12 at the I-495 bridge. There is a faint path on the left side of the bridge that leads under the roadway and down to the shore. The area underneath the bridge is open; covered with small rocks with the minimum amount of brush.

The river is particularly deep at this location. If fly fishing, there is room on the rock ledges that extend into the river that allow for an unobstructed backcast. You need a sinking line to get your lure down as far you need to. If using spin gear, employ the full range of lures -- bring a few deep runners that you can fling out into the middle of the river.

From underneath the bridge looking west, you can see the rock outcroppings in the Carderock area another half mile upstream. It's not worth walking from here to there when you realize you have to walk all the way back to Lock 10 when you are ready to go home. It's much easier to park at Carderock and fish the rock outcropping from there. Besides, the shoreline is densely packed with vegetation making travel difficult.

The view downstream is formidable. The dominant structure is a stark cliff that cuts off shoreline access unless you approach from inland. Therefore, walk away from the river to move around the rock cliffs. Locate the ditch (Rocky Run Culvert -- you can see it on the Google satellite view - 38.970946,-77.177753) that joins the river on the eastern side of the bridge. At low flow, the culvert holds stagnant water and shallows out next to the river. The junction is the easiest place to cross without getting your feet wet.

Follow the culvert back towards the towpath to avoid the massive rock structures near the shore to discover the valleys between the rocks that allow you to crawl to the top and then out on the rock ledges. There is plenty of poison ivy, not only here but everywhere along the towpath, and, by itself, is a good reason to stick to the paths where you can.

Once on the ledge, you can gaze down into the depths of a very deep section that is a productive spot to fish. To continue to fish from the shore as you move back towards Lock 10, dodge around the second outcropping and move back to the river. The shoreline thins out and it's fairly easy walking. Use spin gear anywhere downstream given the closeness of the vegetation on the shore.

If you like fishing here, you may conclude that you can shortcut the walk by parking on the shoulder of the Clara Barton next to Lock 12. At that point, the shoulders are wide and grassy with only a shallow ditch separating it from Lock 12 and the towpath. Unfortunately, parking on the shoulder is illegal and if you do that, expect to get a ticket.

This is the view up to Carderock.

At the back of the picture is the key fishing location adjacent to the Billy Goat Trail.

To the left are the bluffs associated with the Scots Run Nature Preserve on the Virginia shoreline.

The Little Falls gage was 3.28 ft.

This is the perspective looking upstream from the second major rocky outcropping.

The rock ledges are clearly visible in the satellite view on Google maps. Enter 38.969219,-77.177989 and zoom in.

This is the downstream view from the first rocky protrusion east of the bridge at 38.969219,-77.177989.

The best way to fish this section is from a canoe or kayak given the depth of the water and the lack of easily accessible shoreline structure.

There are two good rock ledges that allow you to fish the deeper water.

Bottom line

This is the best accessible deep water near the towpath. Since the river compresses to squeeze through the narrow channel between Virginia and Maryland underneath the bridge span, the depth allows the large volume of water to push through. Not only does that flow create a hazard for the unwary, it carves out an extremely deep cut that requires plenty of weight on your lure to fish properly.

Scotts Run Nature Preserve

Google Map Coordinates: 38.959949,-77.205195

Summary Rating

Pressure	Green	Canoe/Kayak Launch	Red
Physical Fitness	Red	Trailer Boat Launch	Red
Wading	Yellow	Parking	Green
Shore Fishing	Yellow	Regulations	Yellow
Spin Fishing	Green	Fly Fishing	Green
Scenery	Green	Overall	Yellow

Special Regulations

According to section 08.06.01.03 of Maryland law, anglers must wear a US Coast Guard approved personal floatation device while fishing in the river between the base of Stubblefield Falls and the Great Falls Dam.

Please re-read the discussion of the Fairfax County and Northern Virginia Parks Authority regulation before you wade fish in this location.

Getting to the Stream

From I-495, take exit 44 onto Rt 193 north. Immediately after leaving the Beltway, there is a sign pointing to a parking area on the right. Skip that lot and continue down the hill to the second parking area that is east of the stream where the road bottoms out. That turnoff into the nature preserve is approximately 0.8 miles north of the interchange on the right (north) side of the road (38.959949,-77.205195).

There is plenty of parking at this primary entrance to the 336 acre park. Walk to the north end of the parking lot and start down the broad, well marked trail that is part of the Potomac Heritage Trail system and parallels Scotts Run; eventually leading to the Potomac. This is easy walking with the stream on the right and large houses perched high on the bluffs to your left. In fact, it's a good place to use a bike to move quickly to the water's edge. There are two minor obstacles as you walk down the path. Each of these occurs where the stream crosses the trail. The Park Service made it easy to get across the stream without getting your feet wet by building small pilings, properly spaced for walking, that allow you to skip across the stream bed above the water.

There is no choice at the first crossing. Using the pilings, walk across and continue down the trail on the west bank of the stream. A short while later, the trail forks with one fork leading back across the stream and uphill while the other continues north on the west bank. Both trails lead to the same place at the river's edge (38.96772,-77.20227). The trail on the west bank of the stream tightens and narrows with fallen trees requiring detours.

Alternatively, follow the trail across the stream to stagger up and over a moderately steep hill that drops down to the river's edge on the right-hand side of the confluence of Scotts Run with the Potomac. Either way, the walk to the river's edge is approximately 0.75 miles.

Environment and Fish

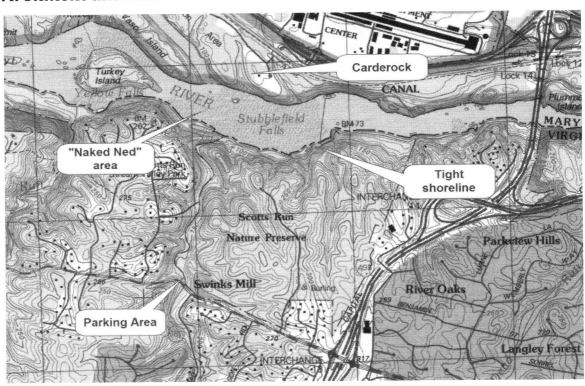

Stubblefield Falls can be problematic depending on the water level. The fact that it is a class III rapid probably should tell you everything you need to know. Be careful if you decide to wade and obey the Maryland regulation that requires a personal flotation device. If you took the trail across the stream, you ended up on the east side of the small waterfall where Scotts Run joins the river. The confluence marks a deep spot that is problematic to wade around. The other, more difficult trail, ends on the west side of the waterfall where there is better access to the upstream section of the river. That said, the shallower areas can be reached by following the trail across the stream. The farther you move up river, the deeper the river becomes.

Stubblefield falls is a mixture of riffles and ledges and is popular with kayakers who make the run down from Anglers Inn to the takeout near Lock 8. Pick your way carefully if you move away from the shoreline. Shoreline fishers have a different problem in that the section of the river downstream from the confluence parallels a steep bank that limits mobility. While you can fish from the shore, be exceptionally careful given the steepness of the cliffs beyond the downstream boundary of Stubblefield Falls. Given the inherent danger associated with Stubblefield Falls, even shoreline fishers should wear a personal flotation device.

Both spin and fly anglers can use their equipment in this location with the caveat that fly gear will not be usable from the shore.

You could drive a truck down the broad trail that leads from the parking lot to the river. The trail remains wide if you follow the branch that goes east across the second stream crossing.

There are two stream crossings, each have pilings that allow hikers to keep their feet dry - even during high water conditions.

This is the view upstream from the confluence of Scotts Run and the Potomac.

To provide a different perspective from the picture shown in the Carderock section, this was taken when the water level measured at the Little Falls gage was 5.34 ft.

Note that all of the subsurface structure visible in the Carderock picture is fully covered with water.

Downstream from the same location.

As anglers, we sometimes tend to be optimistic and may shrug off a high water reading and make a poor choice. Given the visual evidence presented in these two pictures, do not attempt to fish here if the gauge readings are high.

It's just not fishable at high levels.

The waterfall at the end of Scotts Run is a scenic and popular attraction.

Expect to see many hikers in this section of the Park.

You may be tempted to fish in Scotts Run if the water level is high since it has a "trout stream" feel to it.

Scotts Run dries to trickle during the summer months and all you will get if you fish it is practice.

One final comment, there is an elderly gentleman known as "Naked Ned" who busies himself building small dams in the shallows of the river during the summer. He mostly performs this feat, wearing only what he was born with, in the area around Stubblefield Falls. The last known sighting that I am aware of was in late 2008, but he may reappear...

The dilemma of "Naked Ned" emphasizes the jurisdictional issues associated with the river. Since neither the Virginia authorities nor the C&O Canal NHP Rangers have jurisdiction over the river, they cannot go out into the river to arrest this character since he is not committing a felony. It would require a Maryland law enforcement official to float down to pick this guy up.

Bottom Line:

While Scotts Run does provide access to the river, the challenge of fishing in a class III rapid drives the overall rating of this spot to Yellow.

Carderock

Google Map Coordinates: 38.97218,-77.199233

Summary Rating

Pressure	Yellow	Canoe/Kayak Launch	Red
Physical Fitness	Yellow	Trailer Boat Launch	Red
Wading	Yellow	Parking	Green
Shore Fishing	Green	Regulations	Yellow
Spin Fishing	Green	Fly Fishing	Green
Scenery	Green	Overall	Yellow

Special Regulations

According to section 08.06.01.03 of Maryland law, anglers must wear a US Coast Guard approved personal floatation device while fishing in the river between the base of Stubblefield Falls and the Great Falls Dam.

Getting to the Stream

From I-495, take exit 41 onto the Clara Barton Parkway and follow it north. The next exit is Eggert Road. Take it and turn left to go across the bridge over the parkway. Follow the road until it dead ends. There are four different parking areas.

There is nothing tricky about finding the parking lots

Each of the four parking areas offers a distinctly different fishing experience.

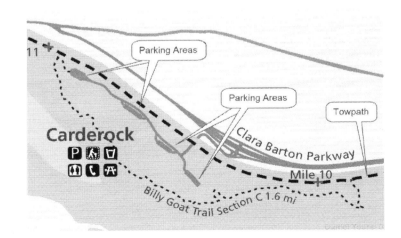

Environment and Fish

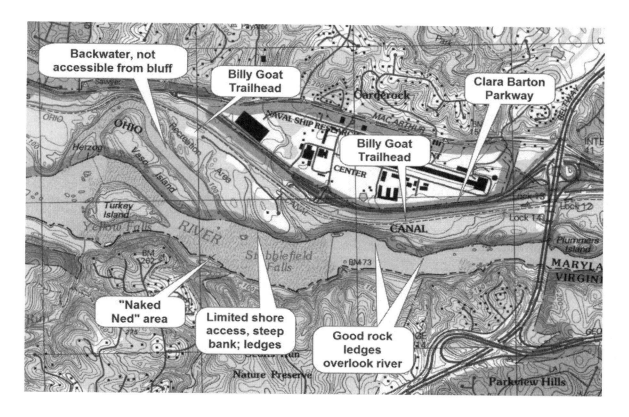

North Area

The westernmost parking area (38.976025,-77.205563) is packed on weekends as a result of its close proximity to the western end of section C of the Billy Goat Trail. Of the three Billy Goat sections, section C is the least strenuous and gets a lot of traffic. Like the others, it offers great views of the river from high places. The fact that it runs along a bluff reduces its utility as a fishing access trail.

To reach the western terminus, leave the parking lot by following the trail adjacent to the public restroom. It makes a sharp turn to the left at the cliff overlooking the side channel of the Potomac running between Vaso Island and the main shoreline. This is not a good place to fish. Getting down to the shoreline involves dangerous climbing to reach an uncertain result. Although I rarely shy away from a reasonable physical challenge, the slack water below was not compelling enough to convince me to override my concerns and climb down. If you were to make the climb, don't bring your fly rod because there is no area for a backcast. Based purely on observation from the top of the bluff, the water appears deep without any attractive smallmouth characteristics like ridges, rocks or significant fallen shoreline structure.

A better choice is to skip this area altogether and move to the middle lot where the trail leads directly to the shoreline and provides good access to Stubblefield Falls.

This is the view upstream towards Vaso Island from the vicinity of 38.97403, -77.20535.

A steep cliff protects the side channel -- there is no safe passage to the shoreline.

The Little Falls gage was 3.29 ft.

Middle Area

Assuming you drove to the western parking lot and peered over the sharp cliffs to verify my assessment of accessibility to the river at the side channel, you may be tempted to park at the next lot east (38.974499,-77.202516) to test access from that location. Don't bother. The lot does not have any defined trails leading to the water's edge and, even if you were to bushwhack through the brush, you would find yourself pulling back in horror from the same set of sheer cliffs you encounter walking in from the western parking lot. Skip this and continue east to the next large lot on the right (38.972572,-77.20052).

This lot overlooks a well maintained picnic area that sits high above the river where it commands scenic views downstream towards the American Legion Bridge. Ignore the picnic area and move along the right-hand (western) side of the open field.

50 yards from the lot, a side trail turns west into a gully next to a sign warning about the dangers of wading at 38.97187,-77.20080. Skip that trail and continue to follow the wood line towards the river.

A couple hundred feet later, a trail dips down a gentle slope next to another sign that cautions about the dangers of wading and quickly puts you at the river's edge.

At the bottom of the hill, the narrow path intersects the Billy Goat Trail that parallels the river and provides access for shore fishing. While the shoreline along this section is compressed with limited lateral mobility, there are places where you can climb down to walk out on rock ledges that stretch for a limited distance into the river.

The shoreline features a mix of deep and shallow areas with good smallmouth holding structure visible just under the surface. Fly anglers, unless they are willing to wade in the class III Stubblefield Falls rapids, are at a disadvantage given the inability to move away from the steep, vegetated bluff that was designed to catch even the most expert backcast. So, use spin gear to minimize frustration if you intend to fish from the shore.

If you wade while wearing your PFD in accordance with Maryland State law, there is a shallow shelf that runs parallel to the shore in this area that permits movement far enough away from the steep banks to use fly gear.

The trail along the shoreline is part of the well maintained Billy Goat Trail network.

There are a reasonable number of opportunities to move down the steep bank to the shoreline.

This is a typical access point that demonstrates the need for careful movement when climbing down to the river's edge.

In addition, there is not much room to maneuver in either direction. Once here, fish that solitary spot and return to the trail.

Using fly fishing gear from the shore would be an exercise in frustration. You need to move out into the river where it is safe to do so.

The view upstream from 38.96983, -77.19917 shows some of the good smallmouth structure defined by gradient breaks, rocks and current eddies.

The river is shallow enough to wade in this location -- wear a PFD!

The Point of Rocks gage was 1.75 ft and the Little Falls gage was at 3.29 ft on the day this picture was taken.

This is the view downstream from the same point towards the rock outcroppings that are accessible from the eastern parking lot.

This is a broad area of shallow water covering a dense rocky bottom.

If you are in a canoe or kayak, you should fish away from the shoreline and target areas that are at least 3 feet deep.

South Area

My personal preference when I fish the Carderock area is to go to the east parking lot (38.970846,-77.198396) and explore downstream. The river opens up with rock ridges running out into the water, permitting the use of fly gear instead of spin. To reach the fishing, you have two choices.

The first choice is to walk to the eastern end of the parking lot and join the Billy Goat Trail where it approaches the lot. Follow it down to the edge of the river. Slide down the steep bank to land on a narrow shoreline next to a broad flat where the water runs fast and shallow. Smaller smallmouth bass will hang in this area in search of baitfish. Fishing in the shadow of the bank limits you to spin gear. But, if you move out on one of the rock ridges just downstream or walk out on the shallow shelf that extends from the shoreline, all bets are off and either fly or spin gear can be put to good use.

Continue to follow the Billy Goat Trail as it moves east, using it as a high speed route to get from one fishing spot to the next. The best places are near the large rocky protrusions that you saw when you looked upstream from under the American Legion Bridge at Lock 12.

The other option from the eastern parking lot is to walk back towards the Clara Barton Parkway. About 50 feet before reaching the bridge, there's an old road running off to the right. Follow its gently upward sloping gradient to join the C&O Canal NHP towpath and turn right to continue east for just under half a mile.

There's a sign posted on the towpath (38.97088, -77.18908) announcing that the well-defined trail behind it is the southern terminus of section C of the Billy Goat Trail. Follow the Billy Goat Trail down the easy hill until it constricts as it enters the heavily vegetated shoreline. At that point, a rocky spur extends out into the middle of the river sandwiched between two shallow, stagnant backwaters. When you see the path hit water, you know you've gone too far -- backtrack and move out on the spur. This ridge extends a good distance into the river, but it is heavily overgrown. You have to fight your way through thick vegetation to eventually perch at the end of the ledge at 38.96895,-77.18833.

The view upstream from the shoreline where the most direct trail from the eastern parking lot meets the river.

You can fish upstream using fly gear once you leave the protective cover of the steep bank on the right.

This is the view downstream from the same spot. While the shoreline is open and unobstructed, the river is extremely shallow.

The Point of Rocks gage was running at 1.72 ft and the Little Falls gage at 3.01 when this picture was taken.

This is the view upstream from the second set of rock ledges along the Billy Goat Trail.

It is actually a bad place to fish in low water as there is little flow over the slick rock ledge; producing a still, deep backwater.

Here is where the fishing gets both good and interesting.

You can work your way out on these rock ledges to fish the faster moving current (vicinity 38.970203,-77.195392).

On this day the Point of Rocks gage was running at 1.72 ft and the Little Falls gage at 3.01.

This is the view from the edge of Billy Goat Trail looking at the same general area, but at a different water level.

On this day the Point of Rocks gage was 1.75 ft and the Little Falls gage at 3.29.

Note that even a small variation in water volume creates a different fishing environment with the slightly higher volume covering many of the ridges.

This is the view of the rock ledge that shows the 500 feet of shoreline you can fish at 38.96895,-77.18833.

From that same rocky perch, the American Legion Bridge looms in the distance.

The shoreline between the ledge and the bridge is thickly overgrown and is difficult to fish without a significant amount of work.

The river compresses and increases its velocity as it makes a run towards the American Legion Bridge.

Bottom Line:

It's a lot of work to get to marginal water at Carderock. Shoreline access is limited and wading can be challenging given the class III rapids of Stubblefield Falls.

Angler's Inn

Google Map Coordinates: 38.981864,-77.226591

Summary Rating

Pressure	Yellow	Canoe/Kayak Launch	Yellow
Physical Fitness	Green	Trailer Boat Launch	Red
Wading	Red	Parking	Green
Shore Fishing	Green	Regulations	Yellow
Spin Fishing	Green	Fly Fishing	Yellow
Scenery	Yellow	Overall	Yellow

Special Regulations

According to section 08.06.01.03 of Maryland law, anglers must wear a US Coast Guard approved personal floatation device while fishing in the river between the base of Stubblefield Falls and the Great Falls Dam.

Getting to the Stream

From I-495, take the Clara Barton Parkway north towards Cardrock. At the end of the Parkway, turn left onto MacArthur Boulevard and follow it for a little over a mile to the Angler's Inn. The ample parking lot is to the left of the Inn.

This is a popular spot for kayakers, hikers and bikers. Outfitters conduct kayak training based out of the parking lot, adding to the congestion. On a nice weekend day, this area fills up quickly.

Follow the beaten dirt road down the hill to the bridge across the canal and onto the towpath. From this point you have several choices. You can move directly down the hill to the river or walk up to the "B" section of the Billy Goat Trail that leads to the base of the Mather Gorge.

Environment and Fish

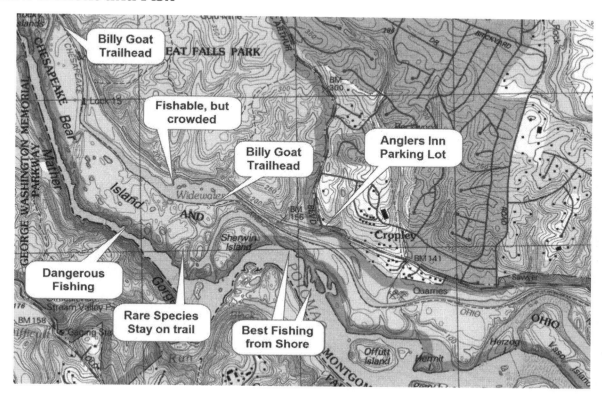

Directly to the River

If you would rather not deal with the strenuous Billy Goat Trail, turn right as soon as you get across the canal bridge and hop on the small trail that moves down the steep hillside to the river. For a larger, more popular path, turn to the left at the bridge and walk approximately 25 yards to discover the broad, beaten trail (38.98113,-77.227782) that kayakers use to drag their boats to the takeout/training beach at the bend in the river.

Both trails put you on a calm backwater; the strength of the current is in the middle and along the Virginia side of the river. Looking up the river, a side channel separates Sherwin Island from the main shoreline. The downstream view reveals a broad sweep of river with an open shoreline that looks kindly on anglers who don't want to get their feet wet.

The rock ridges and open shoreline give ample access to the deep water that is typically unwadeable. If you decide to turn your rod upstream, the terrain closes out quickly once the side channel begins near the island. You have to bushwhack through the heavy underbrush to get to the channel and, once you arrive, it is awkward to cast from the shore. Finally, it's not worth it. Since it is just a side channel, it becomes stagnant at low water levels. With no movement of water, there are not a lot of smallmouth bass tucked back into this cranny.

Therefore, head downstream and target the broad, rock ridge that stretches out in the vicinity of 38.979695,-77.227492. Depending on the water levels, this ridge extends 200 feet or more into the river providing easy access to plenty of good water. If you are a fly angler, this is where you need to go since it is the only place where you will not have vegetation interfering with your backcast. The open terrain, with additional rock ridges, extends another 800 feet down river with plenty of places allowing easier movement.

As a side note, the narrow stretch between Offutt Island and the shoreline is worth fishing. It's marginal for wading, but you can fish from the shore. You can cut over to the river from the towpath at 38.977193,-77.222471.

Given the deep water and the generally restricted shoreline, this is primarily a destination for spin anglers. While fly rodders can find some places to use their big sticks, they are limited and, with other better places to go, why bother?

Upstream from the entry point at 38.98083, -77.22927, the shoreline is reasonably open and accessible.

The channel leading out of Mather Gorge is at the center of this picture.

The Point of Rocks gage was running at 1.75 ft with the Little Falls gage at 3.29 when this picture was taken.

The downstream perspective shows how broad and featureless the river is in this area.

The start of the rock ledges is visible at the center left of the picture; these provide additional access to fish from the shoreline.

As the river charges around the sharp curve coming out of the Mather Gorge, it narrows and gains velocity in the chute between the Virginia shoreline on the left and Sherwin Island on the right.

38.98132, -77.22990, at the junction of the side channel with the main river, is as far up the side channel as you should fish. Not only is it tough going on the shoreline, but the water becomes stale and uninteresting.

Billy Goat Trail

Here's a caveat. I'm covering this section because it is here, but I do not recommend fishing from the one "least risky" (not safe) point where the trail meets the river. The reason is that the trail moves from the main shoreline onto Bear Island. The island is actually property of the Nature Conservancy that has been placed under the care of the National Park Service. As such, it represents a more fragile ecosystem and there are signs posted requesting hikers not leave the trail and risk trampling on the rare plants that have been discovered in this area. In fact, according to the Conservancy, there are 115 different endangered plants and animals on Bear Island. Given the limited area, it has the highest density of rare species anywhere in the world.

To get to the trailhead, walk west from the bridge approximately 1/3 of a mile. You may want to fish a little bit in the Widewater area to the right of the towpath; it does contain fish. However, fishing the Widewater will not be a solitary experience. You will be continually interrupted by the constant, heavy traffic of bikers and hikers on the towpath. This makes it nearly impossible for fly anglers to fish this water since they have to contend with ensuring their backcast does not snag an unwary traveler.

Section B of the Billy Goat Trail is rated as moderately hard and requires scrambling up and down some fairly steep hills on a very uneven trail. It's a good place to hike, but not a good place to fish. If you decide to fish, do not even think about getting in the river. As the water comes bursting out of Mather Gorge, it's deep, strong and violent. A single misstep will result in a tragedy that is certainly not worth the risk when measured against the pleasure of catching a fish.

As the trail winds through the steep, broken terrain, it intersects the side channel at a couple locations, but, as indicated above, it is not worth fishing the side channel if the current is not moving. At the point where the trail turns west and starts to run parallel with the gorge (38.97948, -77.23657), you can claw your way over the rocks to fish the broad pool marking the spinout of the gorge. I do not recommend this – the "rock dance" is not worth it – and the danger makes it a stupid act. I have not fished here for all those reasons.

This is the Widewater area that offers easy shoreline fishing.

If it's busy, fly anglers will find their backcast ensnaring unwary hikers and bikers.

While Maryland does not establish a limit on the number of hikers or bikers you can catch, the fight to land them may not be pleasant.

This is the trailhead for section B of the Billy Goat Trail.

The Park does not allow bikes on this trail; only hikers.

Please carefully read all the advice that is posted on the many signs at the trailhead; particularly regarding physical fitness.

This is a picture of one of the rough spots in the trail. Blue blazes painted on trees and rocks mark the trail.

In many areas, the trail disappears and runs over flat, slick rock surfaces.

From the tip of the trail, this is the view upstream into Mather Gorge.

The terrain is extremely rough with loose rocks and boulders presenting an obstacle that blocks easy movement to the river's edge.

The view downstream from the same location provides additional evidence of the danger in this area. Note the steep, rocky shore -- full of cliffs -- with no easy access to the river.

This was a low water day, but even then, the velocity of the water was crushing and emitted a dull roar as it careened over the downstream rapids and slammed into the bend beyond.

Bottom line

As long as you confine your fishing activities to the Angler's Inn area and do not venture upstream near the dangerous water of the gorge, you can have a decent day here. However, "decent" must include staying on the shoreline.

Great Falls

Google Map Coordinates: 39.00146,-77.246675; 39.002827,-77.256449

Summary Rating

Pressure	Not Applicable	Canoe/Kayak Launch	Yellow
Physical Fitness	Not Applicable	Trailer Boat Launch	Not Applicable
Wading	Not Applicable	Parking	Green
Shore Fishing	Not Applicable	Regulations	Yellow
Spin Fishing	Not Applicable	Fly Fishing	Not Applicable
Scenery	Green	Overall	Not Applicable

Special Regulations

Fishing is exceptionally dangerous in Great Falls Park.

Getting to the Stream

Maryland Side: To reach Great Falls Park, take the Clara Barton exit (41) towards Carderock from I-495 and follow it to the intersection with MacArthur Boulevard. Turn left on MacArthur Boulevard and drive to the Park at 39.00146,-77.246675. There is a fee to enter the Park. The parking lot is to the right of the entrance in close proximity to the scenic areas.

Virginia Side: To reach Great Falls Park, take the Georgetown Pike (VA 193) exit towards Great Falls. Turn right on Old Dominion Drive and follow it into the Park. There are two main parking areas that offer different scenic vistas in the Great Falls area. The lower parking area is at 39.002827,-77.256449.

Environment and Fish

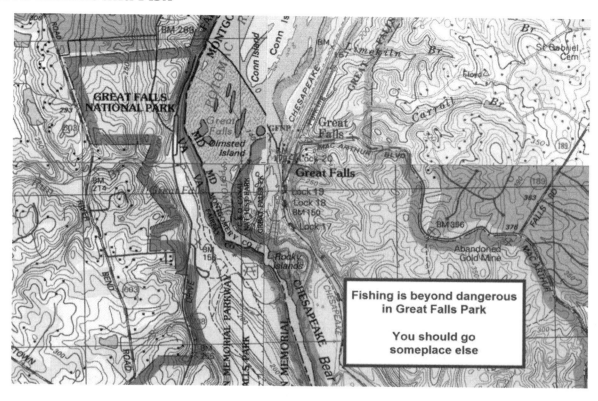

Great Falls is the second largest waterfall in Maryland with a total vertical drop of 76 feet from top to bottom. In traveling that distance, thousands of gallons of fast moving water careen and twist through narrow canyons with slick, steep rock sides. Given that, from my perspective, there is no fishing in either of these locations. The danger is obvious. Do not enter the water or go near the shoreline.

There are people who fish in Fisherman's Eddy on the Virginia side and who use the River Trail that leads upstream from the parking lot on the Maryland side, but, in my mind, the risk is not worth the reward. For that reason, I recommend you visit the parks, but limit your outdoor activities to hiking, biking and taking in the scenic vistas that will surround you.

A final option, that presents moderate risk, is to follow the trail that parallels Difficult Run at the southern extremity of the Virginia side of the Great Falls Park. That trail puts you on the river directly across from Bear Island. As you head north on Rt 193, you will pass the marked parking area for Difficult Run on the left. The actual parking lot (38.978244,-77.24925) is around the corner from where Rt 193 actually crosses Difficult Run. Park in the lot and follow the trail back to the crossing and continue to the river.

This is one perspective of the Great Falls area looking downstream from the Maryland side.

The boiling, fast and violent water is an obvious tipoff that this is not the place to play along the shore or attempt to fish.

The view from the Virginia side is equally dramatic and should deliver the message that this is not the place to fish.

This is "Fisherman's Eddy". As I mentioned above, I have not fished in Great Falls Park since I consider it the beyond dangerous.

Bottom line

Enjoy the view, forgo the fishing.

Riverbend Park

Google Map Coordinates: 39.018317,-77.245844

Summary Rating

Pressure	Red	Canoe/Kayak Launch	Green
Physical Fitness	Green	Trailer Boat Launch	Green
Wading	Green	Parking	Green
Shore Fishing	Green	Regulations	Yellow
Spin Fishing	Green	Fly Fishing	Green
Scenery	Green	Overall	Green

Special Regulations

Please re-read the discussion of the Fairfax County and Northern Virginia Parks Authority regulation before you wade fish in this location.

Getting to the Stream

Take exit 44 from I-495, go approximately four miles and turn right on River Bend Road. There will be a sign for the park. Continue for two miles and turn right on Jeffery Road. Turn right on Potomac Hills Street to go into the park (39.018317,-77.245844) where there is a large Visitor Center that sells a variety of tourist items and some fishing gear. There are good public restrooms as well.

As you drive into the Park, the Visitor Center is on the left with the boat launch at the end of the road. There is a small fee to use the launch. If you intend to wade, take the trail that leads to the left from the boat launch to head for points upstream.

An alternative if you want to make a beeline for the good fishing up river, is to continue on Jeffery Road, not turning off to the left on River Birch Drive, to the Nature Center of the Riverbend Park. You can hike in from the Nature Center to the Potomac Heritage Trail farther upstream from the main facility.

The access trail along the west bank of the river is wide and well beaten. Most of the users of the trail are hikers, not anglers, so do not be discouraged and think you are entering a high pressure area.

Most of the fishing occurs from the shore directly around the boat launch with fewer people taking the time to walk upstream.

Environment and Fish

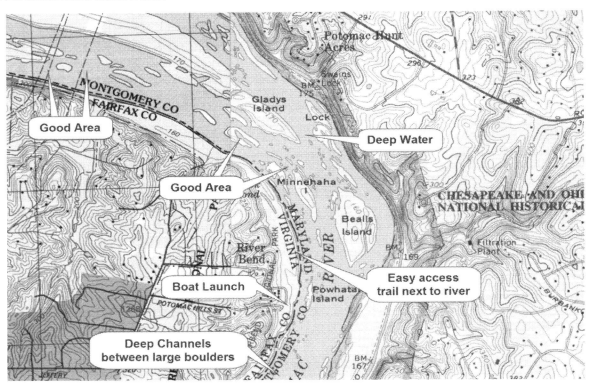

Consistent with every other access point on the Potomac River, you have choices:

- You can work the entire shoreline both up and downstream from the boat launch.
- You can launch a canoe and make a beeline for the good structure upstream or move to the center of the river near the boat launch where there is deep water with large submerged rocks
- You can walk upstream for approximately 1/2 mile and begin fishing in a great, rocky area that is very conducive to wading.

The boat launch at Riverbend is suitable for canoes, kayaks and trailered boats. The danger levels associated with the river are clearly painted on the concrete ramp. If you intend to wade, you should abandon that idea if the water levels are above normal and in the "yellow" area.

You can fish this section from the shore, but you should not go any farther downstream than the tip of Conn Island (39.009622,-77.248542) where the start of the danger area associated with the Great Falls Dam and gorge is marked by a string of buoys across the river.

If you have a canoe or kayak, put in and immediately move downstream to the shoreline at river right to fish the good rock farm that exists in the 200 yards leading up to the buoys. This is a deep stretch of the river, and has noteworthy underwater structure. After fishing downstream, rotate over to the far shore (you can also access this from the Maryland side by walking down from Swains Lock) and fish your way up to Gladys Island. The closer you get to the island, the better the fishing structure becomes.

If you don't have a canoe, while you can fish downstream from the boat launch from the shore, my recommendation is to skip that stretch and walk upriver on the path that starts at the boat launch. There are many places where you can scramble down the steep river bank to get to the shoreline. Recently, the Boy Scouts completed a project to install stairs at key locations to make this easier and safer. The best area to fish if you're confined to the shoreline starts at the base of Black Pond in the vicinity of the downstream tip of Minnehaha Island (39.023668,-77.245892) and extends back to the boat launch.

If you can wade, start here and fish up to the chute between Gladys Island and Watkins Island (39.027552,-77.250495). Another good area, that you can reach on the Potomac Heritage Trail by walking another 1/3 mile, is where the pipeline easement crosses the river at 39.031486,-77.261159.

If you can work your way out to it, the tip of Gladys Island focuses the river into a deep hole that is surrounded by small rock ledges that provide good platforms for standing and fishing. If you are using a canoe or kayak, you can tie it off to the shore on Gladys Island and wade out onto the rock ledges if the water level is correct. There is a great riffle bed to the immediate west of the island where the water tumbles down a small change in elevation, gathers velocity and oxygen and then pours into a deep trench. Upstream and west of Gladys Island, the rock/ridge structure continues and creates a perfect fishing location peppered with cuts between the rocks that lead to deeper holes where fish will lurk; waiting to jump on anything that looks edible.

As a final note, the hike to the upper bend where the natural gas lines cross the river is worth the effort. Hike to this spot earlier in the season before the grass mats make fishing problematic. If you go later, you can use heavier lures to punch through the mats or fish around the edges of the open areas. The experts agree that skidding Zoom Horney Toads, Flukes, or Super Flukes across the mats can cause explosive strikes. Other productive patterns include smaller plastic worms, stick baits or 3" craws and hula grubs.

Both spin and fly anglers will have a good day working this particular stretch. The water levels do not demand an intermediate sinking tip and are conducive to the use of top water presentations such as small size 6 poppers. Spin anglers can use the full range of smallmouth bass techniques in this area.

Although distant, this picture provides a good perspective of the shoreline fishing for the first several hundred yards upstream from the launch.

The brown strip next to the river indicates an open shoreline and easier movement.

This picture looks at the area between Gladys Island on the right and the distant shoreline with Minnehaha Island on the left. There is a good rock farm stretching from the chute to the left of Gladys Island to the shore.

Be sure and fish the deep hole in the foreground that starts at the tip of the island.

The entire area bounded by Gladys Island on the north, Bealls Island on the south and Minnehaha Island on the west offers a great environment for smallmouth bass.

Be sure and look for places where the current pushes water through the channels as opposed to fishing the stillwater if you are in pursuit of smallmouth bass.

This is the view looking downriver near the tip of Gladys Island.

This picture and the one above were taken vicinity of 39.02672, -77.24247

The Point of Rocks gage was 1.13 ft and the Little Falls gage at 3.2 when both pictures were taken.

There are significant rock structures that you can use to move out into the mainstream of the river without having to get your feet wet.

All of these offer good fishing above and below the gradient breaks where the water pushes into the channels between the different rock features.

This area borders the Virginia shoreline only feet from the access trail.

There is a gentle shoreline upstream from the boat launch. The terrain feature on the left of this picture is Minnehaha Island.

With a good cast, you can work this entire channel from the Virginia riverbank.

A kayak or canoe provides your best opportunity to work the varied and interesting structure between the shoreline and Minnehaha Island if you cannot wade.

The Point of Rocks gage was at 1.08 ft; a low level, when this picture was taken. The Little Falls gage at 2.62 ft.

Bottom line

Riverbend offers ideal conditions for smallmouth bass fishing as well as some of the best shoreline fishing on the Virginia side in the lower river. In particular, walk upstream away from the densely populated and pressured area around the boat launch and you can have a good, semi-private day on the river. The farther up you go, the better it gets. If you go upstream, quickly fish your way through the flat water and concentrate on the parallel rock ridges that extend from the Virginia shoreline out to Watkins Island. Each of these creates a riffled and highly oxygenated area that will hold the best fish.

Swains Lock

Google Map Coordinates: 39.031219,-77.243543

Summary Rating

Pressure	Red	Canoe/Kayak Launch	Yellow
Physical Fitness	Yellow	Trailer Boat Launch	Red
Wading	Yellow	Parking	Yellow
Shore Fishing	Green	Regulations	Yellow
Spin Fishing	Green	Fly Fishing	Green
Scenery	Green	Overall	Yellow

Special Regulations

None.

Getting to the Stream

Take the River Road exit onto MD 190W from I-495. Follow River Road for a little over 6 miles and turn left on Swains Lock Road. The road will end at the small parking area.

Many of the books written about the canal mention the boat rentals offered by the Swain family at their seasonal concession located at this lock. Unfortunately, they shut down operations in 2006; ending almost a century of providing that service. The Swain family had worked on the original canal, operated the lock and lived at the lock house since the early 1900s.

Environment and Fish

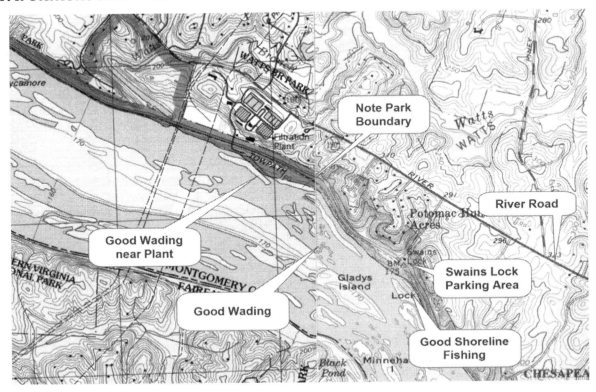

Depending on which way you go from the parking area, you can have a dramatically different day. The best shoreline fishing is downstream where the river backs away from the shore and exposes a shelf. This creates a good rocky structure upon which you can stand and fish into the deeper water. To reach the best fishing, cross the small, stagnant backwater that provides a thin, sometimes dry, separation between the main shoreline and the complex of islands from which the rock structure extends. The rocks border one of the deeper areas in this particular location. Even if you wanted to wade, it is generally too deep beyond the rocks to do that.

Turning your attention upstream, you can fish the shoreline from the steep bank between the parking area and the lower tip of the island (39.031536,-77.246332), but it is heavily pressured and sees extensive use as a result of the small picnic area and campsite.

This is one of the few places where fly anglers can fish with dry feet if they choose to do so. The vegetation thins out along the shoreline and provides plenty of room for a backcast if they choose their spot wisely. If fishing downstream from the picnic area, use an intermediate sink tip or even a full sinking line if the water levels are up. Spin anglers can use anything in their arsenal at this location.

The better approach, once you obtain access to the river by finding a place where you can walk across to the long, unnamed island (a good spot is usually 39.035661,-77.250688), is to fish from that point back down to the lower tip of the island and out in the river wading towards Watkins and Gladys Islands. Be sure and pay attention to the chute (39.030786,-77.248757) between Watkins and Gladys as well as the entire set of parallel rock ridges that extend from the Maryland shore towards those two islands. The best fishing is where the main current flows close to Watkins Island. The closer you can get to the island, the better the structure becomes. However, given the increased water flow, there are deep areas that demand you exercise caution and wear a PFD. If you're willing to walk a little bit farther up the towpath, you should fish the shallow water at the base of the dam at the water filtration plant (39.03782,-77.255162). There are two additional ledges that stretch across the river upstream of the filtration plant, but with the water backed up from the small dam, it's typically too deep to wade.

One additional comment for fly anglers is that there is enough above surface rock structure to provide enticing targets for small poppers and other top water presentations. It's also shallow enough to eliminate the need for an intermediate sink tip, but you may find that one is an advantage if the current is running fast.

This is the view towards the southern tip of Gladys island from Swains Lock. The river gets very deep on the other side of the rock structure.

The rock structure provides a great platform for shoreline fishing.

This is the view looking back at the shoreline near Swains Lock.

Once you're across to the island at the left of the picture, there is ample access to the river on a wide open bank.

The Little Falls gage was at 2.9 when this picture was taken.

The area upstream from Swains Lock contains the rock farm that is the best place to wade.

The numerous rock ridges separate good pools and provide numerous chutes to focus the water and the fish.

Bottom line

Swain's Lock offers a little bit of something for everyone. If you like to fish from the shore, this is one of the better places to do that. A short walk upstream from the picnic area puts you on a nice section of shallow water that provides for a great afternoon of fishing along the rock ridges that create the deeper pools and the fast water near Watkins Island.

Pennyfield Lock

Google Map Coordinates: 39.054901,-77.290428

Summary Rating

Pressure	Yellow	Canoe/Kayak Launch	Green
Physical Fitness	Green	Trailer Boat Launch	Green
Wading	Green	Parking	Green
Shore Fishing	Yellow	Regulations	Yellow
Spin Fishing	Green	Fly Fishing	Green
Scenery	Yellow	Overall	Yellow

Special Regulations

None.

Getting to the Stream

Take the River Road exit onto MD 190W from I-495. Follow River Road for a little over 9 miles and turn left on Pennyfield Lock Road. There are two parking areas. The first one (39.056917,-77.293829) is near the canoe/kayak launch and the second (39.054901,-77.290428) is adjacent to the bridge across the canal. To walk to the river, proceed past the first lot at the sharp left turn at the base of the hill and drive a hundred yards further south to the second lot.

If you have a trailered boat, you'll have a tough time using the boat launch at Pennyfield. Over the years, silt has built up in Muddy Branch and it is a tight squeeze, depending on the size of your bass boat, to fit through the narrow tunnel under the canal. In addition, you'll probably have to hop out and drag it over some of the shallow spots between the launch and the actual river.

The boat launch is at the west end of the first parking lot.

The creek is shallow and boats have to go under the canal through the small tunnel on the left.

While this is not a problem for canoes and kayaks, you should do a thorough recon to make sure your trailered boat will fit.

Environment and Fish

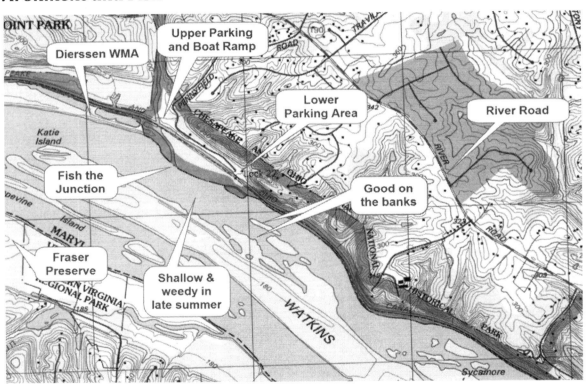

The Potomac is slow-moving and shallow in this wide channel. The main thrust of the current runs on the south side of Watkins Island abreast of Fraser Preserve. If you stand at Pennyfield and look across the river, your view of Virginia is blocked by Watkins Island. However, even though this is a side channel, there is enough water movement to make this a productive fishing destination. At low flows in the summer, the water is shallow; something that facilitates wading until the growth of thick, choking vegetation takes all the joy out of fishing.

This is not a good destination for anglers who want to fish from the shore because the water is so shallow. There is reasonable shoreline access with the trees hanging back just enough from the shoreline to allow you to move easily up and downriver. Unfortunately, there is a wide shelf that extends out from the Maryland shore that minimizes the depth of the water accessible with a cast from the bank.

The best way to fish Pennyfield is to wade. Once out into the river, you face the challenge of "where to fish?" When the river is as broad and featureless as it is in this section, you need to look carefully for the underwater structure. The riverbed is a mix of sand and gravel with enough boulders to make it interesting. There are small ledges that are not big enough to break the surface scattered across the area. Watch for the main flow of the current and focus attention at the boundaries. Even though this section is easily wadeable during the summer, there are some deep holes where a careless step will put you in over your head. As always, wear a PFD to be safe. If the water level is correct, you can fish your way over to Watkins Island and work down the shoreline. Two good spots you should not pass up include the junction of Muddy Branch and the water surrounding the set of small islands downriver from the second parking lot.

There is a tiny island that barely pokes up out of the water at the junction of Muddy Branch. Fish around the island and move over to focus on the junction itself. Muddy Branch dumps colder water into the Potomac and, on hot summer days, the temperature difference attracts fish to the deep, unwadeable hole at the junction. Fish it deep and slow.

Once you finish the junction, wade downstream to the set of small islands. The northern shoreline of the closest small island (39.050985,-77.287703) holds good fish nestled in the tangle of trees that have fallen into the river. The deeper water is along the same northern shoreline. You may have trouble fishing between the small islands and Watkins since it becomes clogged with vegetation later in the summer. In fact, you should not attempt to fish at Pennyfield anytime after early August as a result of the dense vegetation that grows in this area. Since the water is shallow, the vegetation explodes into long, six-foot strands that wave lazily in the slow current to create a huge obstacle to efficient fishing.

While this is not as problematic for fly anglers who can use small poppers targeted at the open holes between the stringy vegetation, spin fishers will have a problem with any subsurface presentation. Given that there are other places you can go on the Potomac where the current is faster and keeps the vegetation cleaned out, you should not fish here once it closes in.

This picture was taken in late September and shows how dense and thick the vegetation becomes.

In fact, it clogs this entire side channel of the Potomac and makes it impossible to fish effectively.

The Point of Rocks gage was running at 1.64 ft and the Little Falls gage at 2.89 ft when this picture was taken.

The downstream view shows that the Maryland shoreline is a little more resistant to the growth of vegetation.

The island on the right is always productive and you should spend some time fishing the northern shoreline.

The small, productive island is on the left with the other islands behind it.

The amount of vegetation increases closer to Watkins Island.

The best time to fish the small islands is early in the season.

Late in the summer, as the sun sets over the Potomac, you can have some great fishing while enjoying pleasant surroundings.

I am amazed that this fishery exists in the heart of one of the major Metropolitan regions on the East Coast.

This is a long view down the Maryland shoreline. Note that the trees are set back from the river and allow shore fishers to move up and downriver easily.

Unfortunately, there are few deep areas near the shore.

Bottom line

The Pennyfield Lock area is worth fishing between May and early August. After that, the vegetation explodes and, unless you are very patient, it is very frustrating to fish. Late in the summer, you'll find yourself spending more time cleaning the weeds off of your lure than fishing.

Seneca Breaks

Google Map Coordinates: 39.067443,-77.328596

Summary Rating

Pressure	Red	Canoe/Kayak Launch	Yellow
Physical Fitness	Red	Trailer Boat Launch	Red
Wading	Green	Parking	Yellow
Shore Fishing	Green	Regulations	Yellow
Spin Fishing	Yellow	Fly Fishing	Green
Scenery	Green	Overall	Green

Special Regulations

None.

Getting to the Stream

Take the River Road exit onto MD 190 West from I-495. Follow River Road for just under 12 miles and turn left on Violettes Lock Road. If you reach the "T" intersection with MD 112, you have gone too far.

Of all the parking areas associated with the canal, this is the most undeveloped. Rounding the corner at the end of Violettes Lock Road, you enter a wide dirt patch with a scraggly tree in the middle. The bridge over the canal is on the right. Park in the dirt area to the left of the entrance. Unlike some of the other parking lots farther down the river, there are limited facilities here although you can usually count on a portable toilet. I feel that this is the most risky place to park in terms of security. Be sure you conceal all valuables in your locked vehicle.

Environment and Fish

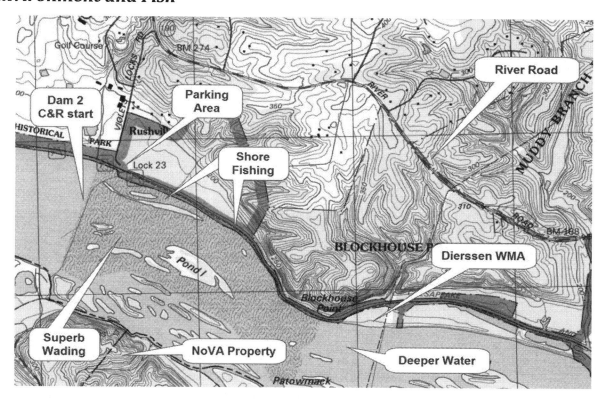

The question that has to be bubbling in your mind is "Why did this get a Green rating?" Granted, this particular access point has plenty of drawbacks in terms of limited parking, no boat launch, slick rocks and other challenges, but they are all overcome by the quality of the fishing.

This is a great place to fish from the shore. You can walk out on the broad rock shelves that line the Maryland shoreline and have instant access to some fairly substantial channels created by the intricate, twisted boulder structure that makes up the Seneca Breaks complex. In addition, you can walk upstream and fish the deep water above the dam without any difficulty at all.

Wading is the way to go here. Once into the Breaks, you have an angler's playground at your feet. But be careful where you put those feet! This entire area is a slick, rocky shelf with the minimum square footage of level ground. You have to watch every step to ensure you do not slip on the slime covered rocks. Look carefully to ensure that you are not about to drop into a deep hole. Over eons of time, water chiseled out deep areas, usually at the base of the cuts between the boulders. Great for fish; bad for movement. This is a prime location to use a wading staff as well as a PFD. In addition to providing buoyancy, a PFD may help cushion a fall when you inevitably slip on the rocks.

The fishable area is just under a half mile square. You can slog all the way over to Virginia or move downstream. The Virginia bank, as discussed in that section of this book, tends to get less water than the Maryland shoreline. If you are here on a low-water day, it's probably not worth the effort to walk all the way over to the Virginia because you will discover that it is a collection of stagnant pools with a pathetic trickle of flow. Stay where the water is running swift and strong.

Even though this is the middle of a rapids, there are broad, deep pools that deserve your focused attention. Fish the current seams and head and tail waters of each carefully. If fishing subsurface, the technique is fairly simple whether you're using spin or fly gear. Flip into the current, let it sink, and twitch every once in a while to give it some life. The hearty bass that live in this challenging environment provide explosive strikes! Fly anglers do not need an intermediate sink tip and should be prepared to flip poppers at likely looking structure.

This is the glorious view out from the upper end of the Seneca Breaks looking towards Virginia when the flow was at 1.23 ft at the Point of Rocks gage.

The Little Falls gage was 3.29 ft.

Note the varied structure, with the large rocks clawing towards the sky, creating random current flows. Fish everything!

The perspective changes dramatically with only a small increase in the amount of water flow. This is exactly why you need to pay careful attention to the gages before you come to the river.

This is essentially the same area as above with flow a little bit higher at 1.42 at Point of Rocks.

Even with water level a little bit above the nominal "normal" upper boundary (2.0 ft) at Point of Rocks, you can see how quickly the structure disappears with additional volume in the river.

The Point of Rocks gage was at 2.48 ft. on the day this picture was taken and the Little Falls gage was 3.05 ft.

While you could still fish from the shore on this day, it was too dangerous to wade.

Finally, even though the water was not officially at the "flood" stage in this picture, you must not fish anywhere near here when the water is high.

The Point of Rocks gage was at 5.28 ft and the Little Falls gage was 4.95 ft.

Shoreline fishers have plenty of "room to roam."

There are numerous rock shelves that stretch out from the barrier islands that provide good access to the deep channels without having to take the extra risk of wading on slick rocks.

There is good shoreline access approximately 0.75 miles down from the parking area (39.062174,-77.318988).

The Point of Rocks gage was at 4.38 ft and the rock ridges running out from the shore are still above water.

The Little Falls gage was 3.33 ft. Odd but true that the Point of Rocks gage was running higher.

If you go over to the Virginia side, be sure and fish the chutes created by the breaks between the islands.

Fish both the entry and exit points.

Float dry flies!

Bottom line

Seneca Breaks is one of the better known fishing destinations on the Potomac as a result of the dramatic, broad and scenic rapids that border Dam 2. The rocky profile creates ideal fishing structure with as many runs and pocket holes as you care to throw a lure at. However, the rapids demand extra caution and you must be aware of and be prepared to fish safely and responsibly – pay close attention to the gage height before hitting the water.

Fraser Preserve and NoVA Regional Park Properties

Google Map Coordinates: 39.051968,-77.334276, 39.045099,-77.31078, 39.031553,-77.277306

Summary Rating

Pressure	Green	Canoe/Kayak Launch	Red
Physical Fitness	Red	Trailer Boat Launch	Red
Wading	Green	Parking	Red
Shore Fishing	Yellow	Regulations	Yellow
Spin Fishing	Yellow	Fly Fishing	Green
Scenery	Green	Overall	Green

Special Regulations

The catch and release area starts upstream of Seneca Breaks (Dam 2). If you fish the dam line, you must release anything you catch upriver from the dam.

You are not allowed to fish from the Fraser Preserve property. However, the public is allowed to use the trails that lead to the river and there is no prohibition on entering the river from this property. Even if the Preserve enacted a prohibition, you can use the Potomac Heritage Trail that runs through the Preserve to move into the Northern Virginia Regional Park Authority property on either side.

Please re-read the discussion of the Fairfax County and Northern Virginia Parks Authority regulation before you wade fish in this location.

Getting to the Stream

There are two green blotches on the map, separated by a small white area, in Virginia across from Seneca Breaks and Pennyfield Lock. If this causes your fishing radar to activate and home in on a potential target, you are heading in the right direction. The Northern Virginia Regional Park Authority owns the two green blotches. The white section is Fraser Preserve and belongs to the Nature Conservancy. All provide additional opportunities to gain access to the river.

Western NoVA Regional Park Property: 39.051968,-77.334276 Drive west on VA 7 from Tysons Corner. Turn right on Georgetown Pike (VA 193) and take an immediate left on Seneca Road (SR 602). Follow Seneca Road all the way to the end. There is a medium sized, dirt parking area to the left of the iron bar gate that blocks further progress down a well maintained asphalt road. That road is used by the County water authority to get to their facilities at the bottom of the hill. Walk or bike down the hill and, immediately before you make a sharp left turn at the bottom, there is an unimproved dirt road leading off to the right. Follow it to the river.

After parking in the dirt lot by the gate, walk or bike down the long, asphalted road until you get to the sharp bend at the bottom.

The unimproved side road is the DC Sewer right-of-way and joins the hardball at (39.057717,-77.33536).

Go around the gate and follow the dim road to the river.

Fraser Preserve: 39.045099,-77.31078 Drive west on VA 7 from Tysons Corner. Turn right on Springvale Road (SR 674). Follow it all the way to the end where it makes a hard right turn (39.03532,-77.309697). At the turn, there is a dirt road with a gate marking the division between the dirt road and the hardball. You are not allowed to drive down the dirt road (even if the gate is open) and must park on the road without blocking the gate or the road. This can be confusing because the sign announcing that restriction hangs from the gate. When the gate is swung open all the way, the sign points across the driveway and is unlikely to be read. There's a small sign on the other side of the gate announcing that you are about to enter "Camp Fraser." A few yards farther down, there is a sign on the right announcing Fraser Preserve. From that point, it is a 0.6 mile walk to the main preserve where the blue trail leads to the river.

At the end of the initial hike from the gate, walk up to the small kiosk on the left at the top of a slight hill that contains a map and additional information on the Preserve. This is the start point for the blue trail. Follow it a half mile through the woods until it intersects the improved dirt road that is the DC sewer system right of way. Walk to the left towards the pipeline easement that runs down a broad, open area. Once you reach the open area, you have moved out of the Preserve and back into Northern Virginia Regional Park property. Follow the beaten trail that leads down the right edge of the easement to the river.

The Fraser Preserve is a 220 acre facility that is open daily from dawn to dusk. It features several trails with the blue trail being the only one that leads to the river or connects with the neighboring Northern Virginia Regional Park Authority property via the Potomac Heritage Trail that parallels the river. Unlike some of the Nature Conservancy properties in other states, fishing is prohibited in the Preserve. Therefore, you're not allowed to fish from the shore and can only use this property to obtain access to the Potomac. To avoid awkward situations, I strongly recommend you not carry visible fishing gear while inside the Preserve. Instead, put a pack rod and the rest of your gear in a day pack where it is not visible. Once you enter the river or leave the Preserve boundaries into the Northern Virginia Regional Park owned property, you can rig everything up and not violate anyone's sensibilities.

This is the entrance to the Fraser preserve from the main road.

Only authorized vehicles can use the dirt road to reach the trailhead; all others must park outside of the Preserve on the road.

Eastern NoVA Regional Park Property: 39.031553,-77.277306 from I-495 take exit 44 onto VA 193 toward Langley and Great Falls. Turn right on River Bend Road and, almost 3 miles later, turn left on Beach Mill Road. Turn right on Carrwood Road and follow it to the corner where it becomes Edmonston Drive. At the corner, there is room for one or two vehicles to park on the side of the road near the locked wooden gate. Follow the unimproved road on the other side of the wooden gate down the hill to where it joins a small trail leading to the right through a draw. The trail ends at the river where it intersects the Potomac Heritage Trail (39.03510, -77.27674) opposite Clagett Island.

Environment and Fish

Western NoVA Regional Park and Fraser Preserve:

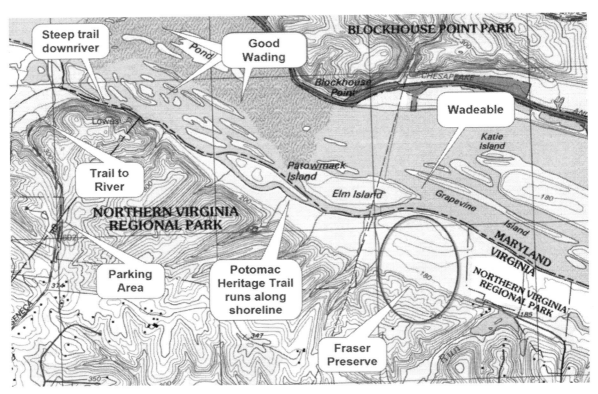

The Fraser Preserve and the Northern Virginia Regional Park Authority properties provide direct access to the river. Unlike upstream, this area is full of long narrow islands that channel the water and make fishing dependent on the vagaries of the current. The boundary between Virginia and Maryland hugs the shoreline except where it swings around Patowmack Island (39.054151,-77.319803; interesting tidbit -- this is the only island in the Potomac that is owned by the State of Virginia.

The river changes dramatically between Fraser Preserve and the upstream section of the Northern Virginia Regional Park. You should not fish the upstream section until you look at it using the satellite view in Google. It's a dense complex of small islands that can be a physical challenge during periods of low water - you could easily become disoriented if you don't pay attention while fishing in the complex. On the other hand, Fraser Preserve lies next to a broad open area punctuated by the long narrow islands that populate the center of the river.

Fraser Preserve

The blue trail leads to the DC sewer right-of-way road and the easement to the river along at the west edge of the Preserve property looking out onto Elm Island. This is a backwater area of the Potomac and the current will be slow and uninteresting. The entire section downstream from this point is better and becomes wadeable at the low point in the summer; reaching about 3 feet deep between the tip of Elm and Grapevine Islands.

To keep from violating the Preserve's prohibition against fishing from its property, you should enter the river and wade out to the other side of Elm Island where you have a choice of fishing down Grapevine Island or walking across Grapevine and fishing in the chutes between Grapevine and Katie Island closer to the Maryland shore. For an additional point of reference, this is the island complex that is upstream from Pennyfield Lock and across the river from the lower portion of the Dierssen Wildlife Management Area.

If you do not want to wade all the way across, follow the Potomac Heritage Trail to the other side of the Preserve where it reenters the Northern Virginia Regional Park Property. The trail extends downriver to the Riverbend Regional Park and you can select any good-looking spot along the way. Watkins Island is the large, wide island that blocks your view of the Maryland shore. There are other smaller, low profile islands that may or may not be visible depending on the water levels. Fishing at the upper and lower boundaries of these islands as well as in the channels between them is always a good choice. Target fast moving water; particularly downstream from the riffled areas.

This is the pipeline right-of-way that creates the western boundary of Fraser Preserve.

Follow the well beaten trail down to the river.

This is the view upstream from the center of the Fraser Preserve at approximately 39.05221, -77.30674. You can see the tip of Elm Island on the left as well as the point of Grapevine Island to the right.

The center of the picture is the lower area around Seneca Breaks on the Maryland shore -- Blockhouse Point.

The view downstream shows Grapevine Island on the left. This entire section of the river is wadeable in the summer.

The Little Falls gage was 4.06 ft when this picture was taken -- well above the normal level for decent wading.

Western NoVA Regional Park - Seneca Breaks

The area around Seneca Breaks is one of the best places to fish in the river. It's a dense complex of rock ridges full of fast-moving water that cuts deep channels leading into pools that can be 5 to 8 feet deep. Obviously, you need to exercise caution - use a wading staff and wear a PFD - but the highly oxygenated water will make it well worth your while.

Entering from Virginia is physically stressful and anglers in poor physical condition should not attempt the hike. In addition to the long walk down the steep hill from the parking area at the northern terminus of Seneca Road (39.05143, -77.33427), you have to scramble over a tightly packed field of slick boulders to reach fishable water.

Early in the summer season, the island complex can be a productive fishing area if there is enough water to make it interesting for the smallmouth to move up the narrow channels. There are numerous, obvious places off of the Potomac Heritage Trail where the water shallows as it sweeps across gradient breaks -- allowing you to move between individual islands.

Once you break through onto the main river, work your way along the rock ridges and target the larger channels that usually lead to and from good holes. Pay particular attention to the shorelines of the islands facing the main current and look for the deep pockets of water sitting just off shore. Your forward motion may be cut off by randomly spaced deep pools. If that happens, backtrack and work your way around using a different rock ridge. Do this early in the season since the Virginia side tends to become a collection of stagnant pools when the flow is at its lowest level in the summer. Use this route to get to the main fishing area at Seneca Breaks as an alternative to parking in Maryland; it will just take more physical effort.

On weekends, the river is densely populated with plenty of anglers and kayakers. However, most of the anglers will tend to stay on the Maryland side because of the half mile walk across the slick surface of the rapids to reach the area around the Virginia shoreline. You may not see anyone else as you move into the island complex on the southern side of Pond Island.

If you decide to follow the Potomac Heritage Trail to the east (down the shoreline), be prepared for a tough hike once the trail transitions to move up the steep embankment that protects this part of the river (39.05847, -77.33176). At that point, the trail moves over tall ridgelines that overlook deep gullies. If you believe that the farther you walk away from the parking lot, the better the fishing becomes, that certainly applies here. The area near 39.05720, -77.32662 is a confluence of many of the channels pouring in from the upstream island complex. The islands become scattered and less dense as you move towards and beyond Patowmack Island (39.054151,-77.319803).

While the discussion above focused on the interesting channels between the islands in the broad sweep of rapids that stretch from their northern boundary to the Maryland shoreline, do not ignore the dam line. The water upstream of the top of Dam 2 (a nondescript collection of rock structure at the top of rapids) is deep and demands to be fished. In addition to smallmouth bass, their largemouth cousins huddle in the deep water immediately upstream of the break.

Although it is not marked on the ground, the boundary between Loudoun and Fairfax counties is at 39.05766, -77.32840; something you should be aware of if fishing regulations change.

If you want to move up or down the shoreline, the Potomac Heritage Trail, marked by green blazes, represents the path of least resistance.

This is the upper part of the Virginia shoreline at Seneca Breaks. Note the pools formed by stagnant pockets of water inside the rough boulder field.

A broader view of the entrance to the island complex on the Virginia side taken from approximately 39.062116,-77.331111.

The Point of Rocks gage was 1.23 ft and the Little Falls gage was 3.29 ft.

Fishable channels occur deep in the island complex off the Potomac Heritage Trail when the river is at higher levels.

This picture was taken at above normal flows and does not represent what this will look like at normal levels when it is safe to actually fish.

The Point of Rocks gage was 2.75 ft and the Little Falls gage was 4.06 ft.

Another view into the island complex.

You can become disoriented once you get into the back channels; it all ends up looking the same.

You should have a GPS or a compass with you to make sure you know the direction of travel to regain your footing on the Virginia shoreline.

Eastern NoVA Regional Park – Clagett Island

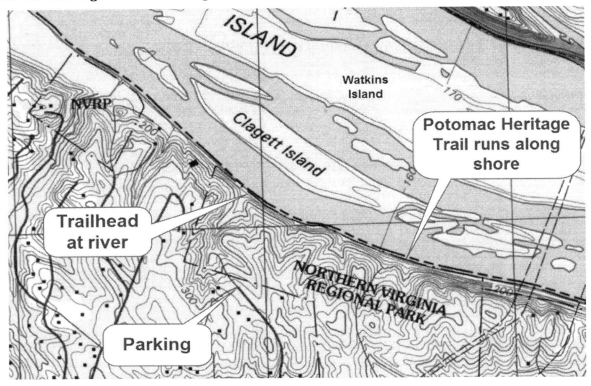

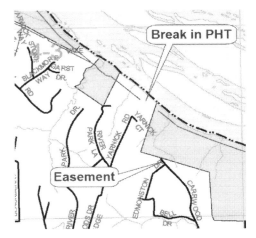

Extract from Fairfax Government
existing trails map

The Potomac Heritage Trail is the one consistent feature that allows you to move along the entire shoreline through Fairfax County. It's a rough, minimally improved trail that leads over aggressive terrain in places.

That said, there is public access to the Potomac Heritage Trail and you can follow it, wherever it leads, without worrying about private property rights... with a couple of exceptions.

Close examination of the Fairfax County Trail map shows that the trail ends for a brief period at the western edge of this property. It then picks up a short distance later.

The other issue is the easement off Carrwood to obtain access to Park property.

The Fairfax County Park Authority easement coordinator was kind enough to do a search for me to determine access rights to this property.

He told me that the outlet road easement "appears as an existing easement on an Amendment to Deed of Dedication and Division dated June 29, 1979." "It is recorded at Deed Book 5216 Page 821 in the County land records."

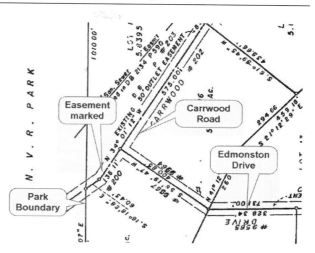

Extract from Deed Book

He continues, "As can be seen on the plat, at the time this document was recorded, the outlet road extended onto the NVRPA property." ... "You will see that the latest tax map still shows the outlet road running to the NVRPA property line." This information is publically available in the County Tax Administration Digital Map Viewer - enter Property Map/Grid 4-3/2009. I also found a record from the Fairfax Board of Zoning Appeals (Page 4, June 28, 1983) that stated:

> "In 1971 the Northern Virginia Regional Park Authority planned to condemn approximately 50 acres of the main tract including the river frontage. To avoid condemnation, a settlement was reached which included a right-of-way to the 50 acres along a route of what is now Carrwood Road."

I called the Zoning folks in Fairfax County and spoke with an Inspector to ask if there were any restrictions on the easement. He told me that the Park is the authority and that there was no other organization I had to check with. All of this leads me to believe that the small easement remains valid. However, you need to make your own decisions and take a copy of this page with you. As a heads up, the property adjacent to the easement had a very loud, large, aggressive sounding dog (as of early 2010). I noticed white flags along the property boundary and those are typically used to mark an electronic dog fence. Take some bear spray with you in case the animal gets out.

Assuming you want to use this access point to get to the river, parking is limited along the shoulder. At most, there is room for two vehicles. Follow the easement down the hill into the NoVA Regional Park property and turn right where it intersects the small trail next to a creek. It's a short walk from there to the river's edge.

The area between Clagett Island and the Virginia shoreline is one of the deeper sections of the river and that severely limits opportunities to wade. You can follow the Potomac Heritage Trail along the river and use it to identify specific locations to slide down the bank and fish. However, the shoreline is overgrown and limits accessibility to those who use spin fishing gear. In short, it's hardly worth the effort to come to this location since the better fishing is almost a mile downriver and is more readily accessible from Riverbend Park.

This is the view looking upstream from the junction of the trailhead leading down from the parking area and the Potomac Heritage Trail (39.035036,-77.276738).

Clagett Island is on the right.

The Little Falls gage was high at 4.06 ft. in this picture.

This is the view downstream from the same location.

The river is wide and featureless in this long stretch.

That does not imply that it is not a good place to fish. Unfortunately, you need a boat to hit this part of the river.

Where you cannot go

Most of this chapter has been about where you can fish. I need to provide a few words about where you cannot go as a result of private property. If you do a thorough map reconnaissance using Google Maps, you may become excited when you see roads leading into other Northern Virginia Regional Park properties that line the river. Other than the places discussed in this chapter, none of the other properties have legal access as of early 2010.

Specifically, Interpromontory Road (39.044786,-77.298367) is a private road that doubles as the access for the DC sewer system when it tracks parallel to the river. After undergoing a few name changes, it joins Beach Mill Road from the north as Bliss Road. There is a sign warning that the road is a private drive. You may also think you can turn from Beach Mill Road onto Clark's Run Road and use that to gain access to the river via the unimproved road you see on Google Maps (39.027052,-77.270451). A quick look at the Fairfax County planned trail map confirms that there is no current or planned access from that point. At the same intersection, Potomac Ridge Road stretches north towards the river and crosses the pipeline easement. You cannot use the easement to get to the river since Potomac Ridge Road is also a private road (39.028319,-77.263005).

The Fairfax County future trail plan documents a few other areas that will be eventually linked with trails that go to the river. As of early 2010, none of these have been created. The website that provides maps and updated information is www.fairfaxcounty.gov/trails/maps.htm. You can download maps that show the current trail network as well as the future planned trails. You should look at this periodically to determine if the County added additional public access points.

Bottom line

The Seneca Breaks is one of the most popular areas to fish because of the fantastic structure it offers. The wide expanse of rapids, coupled with the island complex, presents a varied fishing experience that you can tailor to your physical abilities. You must use a wading staff and wear a PFD because the rocks are slippery and the current can push your feet out from under you.

The Fraser Preserve provides easy access to a decent section if you're willing to hike in from the road. Finally, I recommend against walking to the river from Carrwood since there is no good wading or shoreline fishing where the trail joins the river.

Algonkian Regional Park

Google Map Coordinates: 39.061999,-77.378447

Summary Rating

Pressure	Yellow	Canoe/Kayak Launch	Green
Physical Fitness	Green	Trailer Boat Launch	Green
Wading	Red	Parking	Green
Shore Fishing	Green	Regulations	Green
Spin Fishing	Green	Fly Fishing	Red
Scenery	Yellow	Overall	Yellow

Special Regulations

Maryland enforces a catch and release regulation for all bass between Seneca Breaks and the mouth of the Monocacy River. This park sits at the lower end of the catch and release area.

Please re-read the discussion of the Fairfax County and Northern Virginia Parks Authority regulation before you wade fish in this location.

Getting to the Stream

From Route 7 in Virginia, turn north on the Cascades Parkway at the NVCC Campus. Follow it to the Algonkian Regional Park. Once at the park, follow the signs to the boat launch.

The boat launch borders a wide parking area that extends its reach into broad, grassy fields that are ideal for picnicking.

Environment and Fish

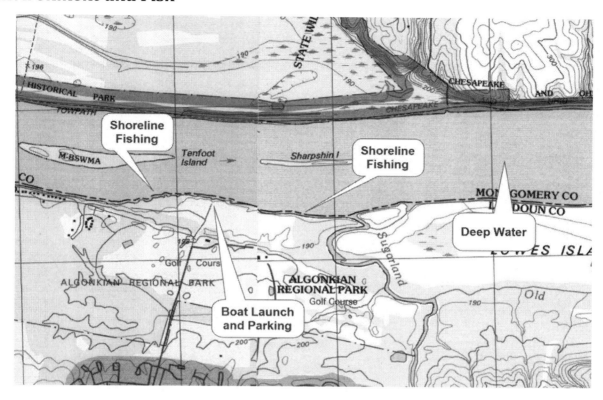

You need a boat to fish the river from Algonkian. Even if you wanted to wade, you cannot because the water is deep along the shoreline. There is a narrow band of ground between the high bank and the river that allows anglers who want to fish from the shore to do so. Depending on the water level, even that brief band may be underwater and you could be stuck standing on the high bank looking at fast water many feet below the edge. If you have time, and are fishing from the shore, walk to the eastern boundary of the Park and fish the spot where Sugarland Run empties into the Potomac opposite of Sharpshin Island. If you decide to fish Sugarland Run, you need a Virginia license.

If you have a kayak or canoe, move directly out to fish around Tenfoot Island just upstream of the boat launch. You can get out and wade around the island at any number of places. Since the island sits in Maryland, there are no restrictions, express or implied, on wading while fishing. The gap between Tenfoot and Van Deventer Island (39.065415,-77.393618) features a shallow shelf that allows you to move around the water.

Finally, the Maryland shoreline, between the tip of Tenfoot and Sycamore Landing Road (39.074477,-77.420182) two miles upstream is both wadeable and productive. Even though the water is flat, there is a fairly quick current that runs about 2 miles per hour in low water conditions. It courses is over a rocky bottom that includes gravel, boulders and deep holes whose existence must be discovered through trial and error. Smallmouth bass love this type of structure and are present in good numbers.

If you fish from the shore, bring spin gear. Fly anglers will be frustrated by the high bank that is a barrier to the backcast. Spin anglers can deploy any type of lure in this area. In late summer, the vegetation grows thick around the Virginia and Maryland shorelines; forcing anglers to target open areas and use weedless presentations. The vegetation will eventually close out access from the shoreline as it creates a thick, impenetrable carpet.

The river is flat and uninteresting.

If you have a boat and can get away from the restricted shoreline, there are plenty of bass on either side of Tenfoot Island.

The view in the other direction is the same.

Below the flat surface, the river features a varied, broken bottom that provides the perfect environment for bass.

The Little Falls gage was 2.85 ft when this picture was taken.

Bottom line

If you don't have a boat, don't waste your time coming here. The shoreline fishing is not worth it when you could go to places downstream with better access and more interesting water. If you do have a boat, it's certainly worth it to put in and fish up the Maryland shoreline as well as around the islands. You can use the boat to get to places where you can tie to a tree and then wade to thoroughly cover the island shorelines.

Sycamore Landing

Google Map Coordinates: 39.074794,-77.420161

Summary Rating

Pressure	Green	Canoe/Kayak Launch	Yellow
Physical Fitness	Green	Trailer Boat Launch	Red
Wading	Green	Parking	Green
Shore Fishing	Yellow	Regulations	Green
Spin Fishing	Green	Fly Fishing	Green
Scenery	Yellow	Overall	Green

Special Regulations

Maryland enforces a catch and release regulation for all bass between Seneca Breaks and the mouth of the Monocacy River.

Getting to the Stream

Pick up River Road from I-495 and head west. Follow it to the dead end intersection into MD 112. Turn left and continue on the road across Seneca Creek for several more miles. Ignore the left turn to the Seneca Landing boat launch. Turn left onto Sycamore Landing Road. The road ends in a small parking area with the trail to the towpath and the river leaving from the south end of the lot.

This is a public hunting area so you should wear something orange if you fish during the hunting season.

If you intend to launch a canoe here, you have to carry it down a steep, muddy bank to the river. The bank consists of soft, slick mud that will form a semi-permanent coating on the bottom of your canoe or kayak. The silty bog continues out into the river for 5 to 10 feet and then switches to a more smallmouth friendly rocky/gravel bottom. In addition to getting your kayak dirty, the mud is treacherous and is more akin to ice than dirt. Be exceptionally careful if you're wearing felt or flat soles; dig your feet in and test each step or you will find yourself taking what could be a bad spill.

Go through the locked gate to the towpath to discover the gap between the trees framing the opening to the river.

While there are a few steps leading down to the river's edge, it's a scramble in the slick mud to get your canoe or kayak to the edge of the river.

Environment and Fish

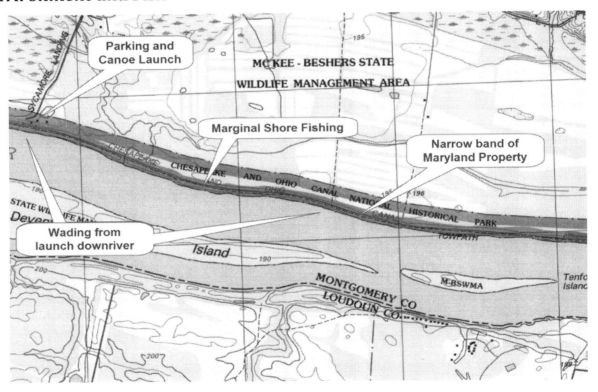

There is not much to see in this section. The river is a broad sweep of calm water lined with thick stands of trees on either bank.

Once in the river, work your way up along the shoreline back towards the launch point. There's a wide seam of shallow water that extends for over a mile from just upstream of the canoe launch to the downstream tip of Tenfoot Island. However, you need to be cautious since there are deep pockets interspersed throughout this entire area. While the bottom is a mix of mud, sand and gravel, deeper areas occur where the river has been able to gouge holes in the sandy areas. There are no rock ledges to target. As you walk, every step kicks up a plume of silt that drifts downstream. Therefore, your best strategy is to work upstream throwing quartering casts to the side where the bottom will still be undisturbed.

That's perfect anyway since you should fish the trenches from the side. This is the place to use weighted lures to get down into channels that run between 5 and 8 feet deep. Given the depth of some of the holes, you must wear a PFD to remain safe. Be sure and mark your path (either mentally or using your GPS tracking function) so you can find your way back if you end up between 2 trenches. Even though the bottom is not slippery, you should use a wading staff to test the depth in front of you as you move. Some of the drop-offs can be steep and abrupt.

The only landmark visible in this stretch is a sunken log that protrudes a foot out of the water just downstream of the parking lot. Even though everyone fishes that spot, fish continue to collect there and are ready to react to anything that floats by. Chalk it up to catch and release!

For boaters, this is a fish-through spot. You'll see plenty of people fishing from boats as they drift downriver in the gentle current; casting to the left or right. It's classic "float by" fishing. While boaters may only get a cast or two at the deeper runs and ledges, you will be able to work them thoroughly given your slower progress through the water.

This is not a good location to fish from the shore. There is plenty of vegetation that obstructs access and the bank against the towpath is steep. There are few areas of level, dry footing at the water level.

The current moves slowly through this section and, when combined with the shallow water, creates an environment where the vegetation grows thickly. Don't plan on fishing anytime after mid-August. In a normal year, the vegetation will have grown to the top of the water and totally obstruct the surface. You can't even get out in a canoe without having to pull your way through thick weeds. While the fish are still here, the extensive, thick and unending vegetation makes this an unattractive place to fish. If you have the time and energy, you should come out at the end of August or September with a pair of binoculars to observe the river. The open areas, devoid of vegetation, are where the deeper trenches exist. Mark those for the future.

You can use either fly or spin gear with spin anglers having the advantage. Given the wide open nature of the river and the need to cover a lot of territory to find the trenches and the deep areas, spin gear allows for longer casts that cover more water in the same amount of time. In addition, once you discover the trenches, spin gear has more options for heavily weighted lures to get down to the bottom. No matter what type of gear you use, you will end up throwing in a searching pattern as you look for the trenches. Once you catch a fish, stop and work that location thoroughly! Fly anglers should not plan on using top water presentations unless they see fish feeding on the surface. Instead, put on that sinking tip and get your fly to the bottom.

This is the view upstream from approximately 39.073578,-77.418251.

The small brown spot you see at the center left of the picture is the solitary log that always holds fish.

The view downstream from the same location reveals that there is nothing remarkable or interesting to look at in this section of the river.

It's wide and shallow; making it the perfect place to clog up with thick, weedy vegetation towards the end of the summer.

The Little Falls gage was 3.37 ft when this picture was taken.

Bottom Line

There is plenty of wadeable water. Once in the river, you need to be careful because the bottom is not level; there are numerous trenches and potholes. Even though this is a benign looking stretch of the river, you need to use a wading staff and wear a PFD.

Edwards Ferry

Google Map Coordinates: 39.103406,-77.473108

Summary Rating

Pressure	Yellow	Canoe/Kayak Launch	Green
Physical Fitness	Green	Trailer Boat Launch	Green
Wading	Yellow	Parking	Yellow
Shore Fishing	Green	Regulations	Green
Spin Fishing	Green	Fly Fishing	Yellow
Scenery	Yellow	Overall	Yellow

Special Regulations

Maryland enforces a catch and release regulation for all bass between Seneca Breaks and the mouth of the Monocacy River.

Getting to the Stream

From I-95, turn west on River Rd (MD 190). Follow it for approximately 17 miles and then take a slight right on Mt Nebo Road. Mt Nebo intersects West Offutt Road; continue on Offutt until it dead ends at Edwards Ferry Road. Turn left on Edwards Ferry and follow it to the launch area (39.103406,-77.473108).

This is the view of the Edwards Ferry boat launch from across the river at Goose Creek.

Note the relatively open banks on either side of the launch and the thick vegetation in the foreground of the picture at the junction of Goose Creek.

Shoreline anglers can move a good distance in either direction from the launch.

Environment and Fish

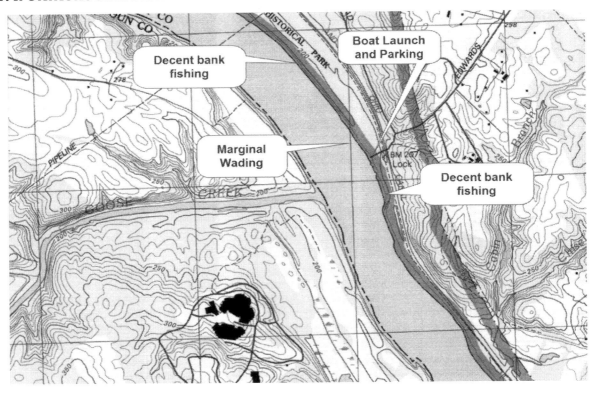

From a wading perspective, Edwards Ferry is not an optimum location. While you can move away from the shoreline, the river drops off quickly the farther you move into the river. It doesn't take much of a drop-off to close out access -- once the river gets between 3 and 4 feet deep, your ability to move is limited. The wading disadvantage flips to become an advantage for anglers who want to fish from the shore.

Since the river drops off fairly close to the shoreline, you can fling lures a good distance into deeper water. Based on the restricted distance you can move into the river, this location is better for anglers who rely on spin gear than a fly rig. While fly anglers can get far enough out into the river to fish without seriously disrupting their backcast, they may find movement a little cramped as they are forced to walk around the deep spots. If you fish this area with a fly rod, be sure and use a sinking tip. You don't need a full sinking line but you do need to get your fly down to the bottom. As summer progresses, the vegetation around the shoreline thickens and provides an opportunity for fly anglers to use poppers and other surface lures. For spin fishers, this is where you can deploy some top water plugs designed for open areas as well as buzz baits.

This is the view up the river from the boat launch. Note how wide and featureless the river is. All of the structure is underwater. There is a shallow shelf that extends into the river from the shoreline until it drops off into a deeper channel.

Depending on the water level, you may or may not be able to get that far out.

This is the view downriver from that same location.

You can wade along the shoreline and fish the overhanging structure or throw at the deep channel towards the center of the river.

The Point of Rocks gage was running at 1.16 ft when this picture was taken and the Little Falls gage was 2.82 ft.

Bottom line

Granted, between Sycamore Landing and Point of Rocks, there are not many options for wading. If you don't have a choice, this is better than not going fishing. Depending on the water level, you can actually have a good day here if you work down the shoreline and look for the fish hanging under the shade trees that line the banks. This is certainly a place you need to fish at least once and see how it works out for you. You may conclude that you are better off going upstream to Point of Rocks or Lander.

Bles Park, Elizabeth Mills Riverfront Park, Goose Creek

Google Map Coordinates: 39.069579,-77.448635, 39.087386,-77.474685, 39.098453,-77.49427

Summary Rating

Pressure	Green	Canoe/Kayak Launch	Yellow
Physical Fitness	Yellow	Trailer Boat Launch	Red
Wading	Green	Parking	Green
Shore Fishing	Green	Regulations	Green
Spin Fishing	Green	Fly Fishing	Green
Scenery	Red	Overall	Green

Special Regulations

Maryland enforces a catch and release regulation for all bass between Seneca Breaks and the mouth of the Monocacy River.

Goose Creek and Broad Run are in Virginia and require a Virginia fishing license. There is no reciprocal arrangement with Maryland once you enter the mouth of the creek.

None of these parks are part of the Northern Virginia Regional Park Authority system.

Getting to the Stream

All three locations are in close proximity to each other and are connected by the Potomac Heritage Trail.

Bles Park: From the Beltway, take Rt 7 towards Leesburg. Alternatively, take the Dulles Toll Road and turn north on Rt 28. Turn left from Rt 28 onto Rt 7. Once on Rt 7, turn right on George Washington Blvd. Turn right on Riverside Parkway. Follow Riverside Parkway to the end where there is a large parking area on the right (39.069579,-77.448635) adjacent to where the Parkway makes a sharp 90° turn south. Follow the trail to the Potomac River and Broad Run. Be sure you get on the correct trail. There are two that leave the parking area. Take the one that is next to the playground, not the one that leads across the open field – it dead ends on a residential road.

Elizabeth Mills Riverfront Park: From the Beltway, take Rt 7 towards Leesburg. Alternatively, take the Dulles Toll Road and turn north on Rt 28. Turn left from Rt 28 onto Rt 7. Once on Rt 7, turn right on Belmont Ridge Road/Xerox Training Center. Follow it to Riverpoint Drive; turning right onto Riverpoint.

Turn left on Squirrel Ridge Place. The road winds, seemingly forever, through a housing area, but don't be confused; you are in the right place. Squirrel Ridge Place is a cul-de-sac. Once you enter the cul-de-sac, turn right on the small road that leads to the east. It joins an unnamed road that overlooks the golf course. Turn left and go to the parking area (39.087386,-77.474685) at the end of the street. From there, you can pick up the trail across the golf course to get to the river. The trail follows the gold cart path past the restroom and through the golf course. It is well marked with signs for "Riverfront Park." Once on the Potomac Heritage Trail, you can move up and down the river. I do not recommend remaining on the cart path to walk up to Goose Creek since you will probably get dinged by a golf ball.

Goose Creek: From the Beltway, take Rt 7 towards Leesburg. Alternatively, take the Dulles Toll Road and turn north on Rt 28. Turn left from Rt 28 onto Rt 7. Once on Rt 7, turn right on Belmont Ridge Road/Xerox Training Center. Follow it to Riverpoint Drive; turning left onto Riverpoint. Follow Riverpoint to the entrance to the Kephart Bridge Landing Park. Turn left from Riverpoint (in the middle of a residential street at 43942 Riverpoint) to enter the parking lot (39.098453,-77.49427). It is very easy to drive by the entrance. Look for 43940 Riverpoint; the "driveway" to the park is sandwiched between 43490 and 43494.

Environment and Fish

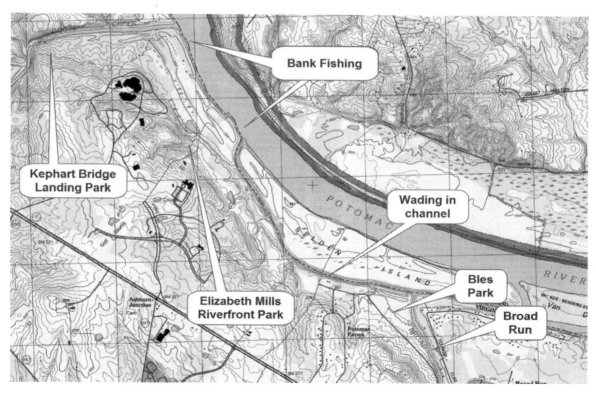

Interesting that the USGS map sheet shown above is so out of date. This area is heavily built up with housing and other development that is invisible on this map.

The Potomac Heritage Trail connects all three properties. This includes a mile long section of the trail that leverages a public easement through the Janelia Farms Medical Research Facility connecting Bles Park with Elizabeth Mills Riverfront Park. In addition, the trail extends upstream from the Kephart Bridge Landing on Goose Creek to connect with Keep Loudoun Beautiful Park that is tucked under the Rt 7 overpass. If the water level is good, you can fish all the way up from Kephart to Rt 7 and beyond. Back on the Potomac, the small side channel between Selden Island and the Virginia shoreline provides good opportunities for wading.

Bles Park

Bles Park is nice park that sprawls over 124 acres and includes a 94 acre undeveloped area featuring walking trails along Broad Run and the Potomac. The Potomac Heritage Trail leverages the Bles Park property to continue upstream through Janelia Farms and extends for 2 miles along Broad Run. From a fishing perspective, Bles Park gives you two options.

The first is to leverage the Potomac Heritage Trail to access the shallow side channel of the Potomac that separates Selden Island from the Virginia shoreline. It may be touch and go wading in the channel with the best opportunity being when the Point of Rocks gage reads 1.6 feet or below. As you work your way up river, pay particular attention to the good holes around the bridge that connects the island with the shore. In addition, there are several small creeks that ease their way into the river from the south creating additional hotspots.

The second option is to fish Broad Run during periods of high water. Broad Run requires a Virginia license and the shoreline can be challenging since it is overgrown with thick, dense brush.

This is the view upstream from 39.07209,-77.44886 where the trail first meets the river.

The water was running high when this picture was taken and demonstrates the need for caution when the river is running above recommended levels.

The river was running at 5.34 ft at Little Falls gage - far above recommended level of 3.1 ft.

This is the view downstream at the junction of Broad Run with the Selden island bypass (39.07110,-77.44448).

At higher water, Broad Run provides decent smallmouth fishing.

This picture was taken when the river was running high. The actual conditions you will encounter on a normal day will show a narrower stream.

The path along Broad Run is wide and well developed. You can ride your bike on this path to move quickly from place to place.

Elizabeth Mills Riverfront Park

Elizabeth Mills contains 122 acres of woods spread along the river and includes the Kephart Bridge Landing access point for canoeing and wading on Goose Creek. Once you park, walk through the golf course on the trail that connects the parking area with the Potomac Heritage Trail along the river. Make an immediate beeline to the corner where the Potomac branches to run into the small side channel that separates Selden Island from the Virginia shoreline. To move directly to the corner, cut across the field beyond the kiosk that marks the entrance to the park area.

After you fish that spot, either move farther down the side channel towards Bles Park or work your way upstream to the mouth of Goose Creek. There are limited opportunities for wading from the tip of Selden Island upstream since the river is deep. The good news is that the Potomac Heritage Trail provides easy walking as you scout the shoreline. You may have to dodge a few golf balls since the trail runs close to the edge of the course.

Based on that, this section of the river is more appropriate for spin fishers rather than fly anglers. The high banks and thick vegetation are obstacles to a normal fly fishing backcast and optimize conditions for spin gear.

The Potomac Heritage Trail parallels the river, running around the golf course to eventually turn up Goose Creek and connect with the Kephart Bridge Landing access point.

The parking lot borders the golf course.

Walk past the restroom (building in the picture) and follow the signs, staying on the cart path, until you reach the river.

This is the view downstream from the corner where Selden Island (the tip of land to the right) intersects the Potomac River.

This picture looks downstream into the gap between Selden Island and the shore.

On the day this picture was taken, the river was high 5.34 ft at the Little Falls gage.

Goose Creek

The Kephart Bridge Landing is the primary access point for Goose Creek. The parking area is approximately 200 feet from the creek and that distance is something you should consider if you intend to launch a canoe or kayak. Downstream from the parking lot, the creek deepens; limiting the opportunities to wade. There is a broad, shallow, wadeable shelf that extends a quarter-mile downstream that allows you to target the western (deeper) bank of Goose Creek. The Potomac Heritage Trail runs along the eastern bank and provides the gateway to additional locations. However, the banks are steep, the access points are limited and, once in the creek, your movement is constrained to a small area. You cannot walk along the creek bed for an extended distance. Instead, you must enter the creek, fish, climb out and repeat that process as you work your way to the Potomac.

The closer you get to the Potomac, the deeper Goose Creek becomes. There are substantial amounts of vegetation along the shoreline that create obstacles for fly anglers who are confined to small spaces near the shore as the creek deepens. Those same spots provide opportunities for spin fishers who can crawl down to the creek and throw long casts targeting the shoreline structure and the deeper middle section.

Upstream from the access point, opportunities for wading improve but the quality of the fishing is directly proportional to the amount of water in the creek. At the height of summer, the creek becomes slow moving with a minimal amount of water pushing downstream. In addition to Kephart Bridge Landing, you can also obtain access at the Keep Loudoun Beautiful Park underneath the Rt 7 overpass and fish up or downstream from that location. It's worth fishing all the way up to that point and beyond if the water levels permit. Although I have not been this lucky, others have reported catching smallmouth that weigh in at 2+ pounds in this area.

At the Kephart access point, the creek forms a decent pool along the western bank. The shallow shelf extends a quarter-mile downstream and allows easy wading access in that area.

Moving upstream, there is a nice set of riffles and rapids (39.099044,-77.496164) created by the small drop in elevation between the Riverside Parkway overpass and Kephart Bridge Landing.

The Goose Creek gage near Leesburg was running at 13 cfs (below normal) when this picture was taken.

The east bank is at the left of this picture. Note the densely packed trees overhanging the shoreline.

The west bank is not accessible since it borders private property.

This is the view of the entrance to Goose Creek from across the river at the Edwards Ferry access point.

The Potomac Heritage Trail runs along the shoreline at the left. You can work your way down to the bank at the junction and fish the deep hole that exists there. The Virginia shoreline becomes clogged with vegetation late in the summer.

Bottom line

This area is worth fishing earlier in the season when the water levels push enough volume down the side channel to attract fish. The Virginia shoreline becomes clogged with vegetation later in the summer.

Red Rock Wilderness Overlook Regional Park

Google Map Coordinates: 39.112955,-77.510063

Summary Rating

Pressure	Green	Canoe/Kayak Launch	Red
Physical Fitness	Green	Trailer Boat Launch	Red
Wading	Red	Parking	Green
Shore Fishing	Green	Regulations	Green
Spin Fishing	Green	Fly Fishing	Red
Scenery	Yellow	Overall	Red

Special Regulations

Maryland enforces a catch and release regulation for all bass between Seneca Breaks and the mouth of the Monocacy River.

Please re-read the discussion of the Fairfax County and Northern Virginia Parks Authority regulation before you wade fish in this location.

Getting to the Stream

North: Follow US 15 South from Point of Rocks into Leesburg. Turn left on Edwards Ferry Road (SR 773) and follow it for approximately 1.5 miles.

South: From the Leesburg Pike (VA 7), merge onto VA 267 by following the signs to Dulles Airport. Take exit 1B onto the Leesburg Bypass (US 15 North). Stay on US 15 for just under 2 miles, make a right turn on Edwards Ferry Road and follow it for approximately 1.5 miles.

Be alert for the small sign marking the entrance to the Red Rock Park on the left-hand side of the road. It almost looks like you are turning into somebody's driveway since the entrance is narrow and there are buildings to the left of the entrance at the edge of the street.

Jog left as you turn into the 67 acre park to avoid going into the driveway that leads to private property on the right. The parking lot is in the center of what appears to be a courtyard created by the shells of several old historical buildings. The trail to the river is at the left-hand corner of the open area as you face the kiosk at the north end of the parking lot. It's a short 0.3 mile walk to reach the river's edge along a winding, open path.

This is the entrance to the trail that leads to the river at the upper left hand part of the parking area.

The trail is marked with white blazes and it is easy to see when it is not covered with fall leaves.

The trail takes a steep pitch down at the escarpment overlooking the river but remains relatively easy to negotiate.

The trail joins the river at the upper end of the public property. The private property is clearly and diligently marked by a huge number of bright yellow "posted" signs.

You can fish downstream and remain in the park.

Environment and Fish

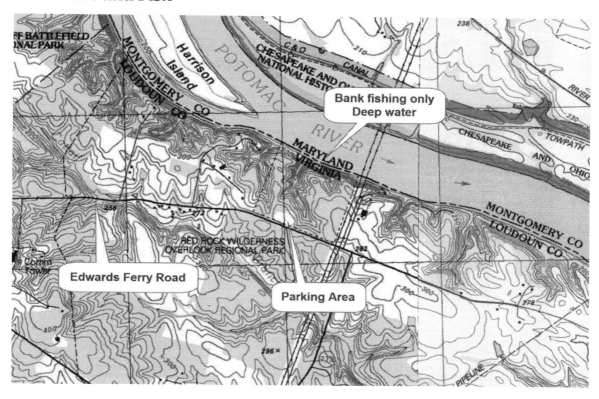

When you reach the river, you could easily believe you are in a formal, manicured park given the broad, level shoreline that stretches in both directions. There are very few fallen trees and almost no undergrowth to claw at your legs; delaying movement up or downstream. There is a small, beaten path that leads along the shoreline, but given the openness of the area, your movement is not restricted to the path.

At typical water levels, the water is deep next to the shore and prohibits wading. If you insist on wading, you will find a muddy bottom with only a few places where you can step off the shore. Even then, your movement from the shoreline will be measured in feet, not yards, since the water gets deep quickly. This is the ideal place for people who want to fish from the shore. There is plenty of structure collapsed into the river with trees throwing wide bands of shade across the water to provide a refuge for bass on hot, bright summer days.

You can fish your way all the way to a steep rock cliff that cuts off access for all but the especially nimble (39.11595, -77.50689). Those brave souls can scramble across the front of the rock face where it pitches slightly out to form a skinny shelf, but be prepared to slide on the slick rocks and take an unplanned bath in the river. The other option is to climb around the steep escarpment from which the cliff protrudes and continue fishing downstream. There is still a thousand feet of park property downstream from the cliff.

Red Rock is not appropriate for fly anglers. The deeply wooded shoreline prevents any effective backcast. The tall trees hang over the water up to 20 feet in places; creating an equally formidable obstacle to your forward cast.

This is prime spin fishing territory. With spin gear, you can flip lures, without limitation, at targeted spots under the tight cover. Since the water is deep, your choice of lures is not restricted to a weedless presentation.

This is the glorious view that awaits you once you negotiate the steep embankment at the end of the trail.

The manicured, park-like nature of the open area provides easy movement along the shoreline from the trailhead to the cliff face approximately a quarter of a mile downriver.

Looking upstream from 39.11702, -77.50965, the river is broad and deep as it heads around the corner to Whites Ferry.

The entire shoreline is sheltered by large trees cocked at alarming angles; stretching their protective branches down to the water's edge.

The view downstream from the same point reveals no compelling rock structure to attract interest.

The shoreline vegetation remains consistent and thick.

The Point of Rocks gage was running high at 2.7 ft on the day this picture was taken and the Little Falls gage was 3.95 ft.

This is the cliff face at 39.11595, -77.50689 that cuts off movement along the shoreline.

The park property continues another thousand feet downstream of this landmark and you can either scramble across the cliff face or climb around on the other side.

Bottom line

This area is not heavily fished given the walk to the water, the short amount of shoreline that is public property and the depth of the water that restricts wading. It is a good place to go if you want to fish from the shore and are not looking for a location where you can spend the entire day. Given the limited fishing opportunity, this location is not high on my list of places to visit.

Balls Bluff Battlefield and Edwards Landing Parks

Google Map Coordinates: 39.13026,-77.530797, 39.120605,-77.525132

Summary Rating

Pressure	Green	Canoe/Kayak Launch	Red
Physical Fitness	Yellow	Trailer Boat Launch	Red
Wading	Red	Parking	Green
Shore Fishing	Green	Regulations	Green
Spin Fishing	Green	Fly Fishing	Red
Scenery	Yellow	Overall	Red

Special Regulations

Maryland enforces a catch and release regulation for all bass between Seneca Breaks and the mouth of the Monocacy River.

Please re-read the discussion of the Fairfax County and Northern Virginia Parks Authority regulation before you wade fish at Balls Bluff.

Getting to the Stream

Balls Bluff Battlefield: From Leesburg, turn east onto Balls Bluff Road from US 15. It dead ends into Balls Bluff Road NE. Turn left and go through the cul-de-sac onto the dirt road that leads to the parking lot in the center of the park (39.13026,-77.530797). There is a sign on the right at the end of the cul-de-sac that reassures you that you are about to enter the park and not somebody's driveway.

Balls Bluff and Edwards Landing Parks merge together with connected trail systems. Of the two, Balls Bluff has a better mix of trails as shown on the official map below.

From the Balls Bluff parking lot, the best trail to the river is the red trail that starts from the northeast end of the parking lot. Be sure you pick up the trail as it leaves the parking lot on the left since that is the direct route to the river. If you accidentally take the trail from the right side of the parking lot, you will get to the same place; it will be a longer walk.

The trail is well marked with red blazes on trees as it leads down into a draw where the trail crosses a small bridge. Aggressive anglers may be tempted to jump off the trail at that point and walk down the creek bed to get to the river. Talk yourself out of that idea since there is an ample amount of deadfall that has built up and blocks progress towards the river. Even though the trail goes uphill after the bridge, it's not steep; it levels out quickly, and puts you on the river in another 50 yards.

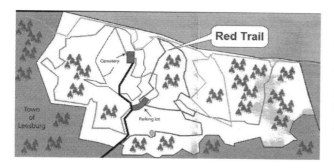

Pick up one of the official maps at the kiosk in the parking lot.

The red trail offers the most direct route to the river. The yellow trail goes to the bluff overlooking the river and it is more difficult to get down to the riverbank from that location.

Once on the river, there is a nice, well defined trail that runs along the bank for most of the shoreline in the Park.

Edwards Landing Park: To reach this small, 32 acre Park from Leesburg, take Edwards Ferry Road east from US 15. Turn left onto Battlefield Parkway Northeast followed by the first right onto Woods Edge Drive. Turn right onto Powhatan Ct. The parking area is on the right (39.120605,-77.525132).

If you park at Edwards Landing, there is a half mile walking trail that goes directly down to the Potomac River. To reach this trail, walk directly away from the pavilion through the chained gate and follow that road until it intersects the Potomac Heritage Trail. Be alert for the green blazes.

Once on the trail, follow it down the hill into a deep cut. At this point you have two choices. You can continue to follow the Potomac Heritage Trail across a small wooden bridge and then up the steep hill to your front or turn right and follow the crack between the two ridges. If you stay on the trail, you will have to veer right once you go over the ridge and reach the bottom of the next draw. At that point, the trail lurches uphill to follow the bluff west along the river. Instead of staying on the trail and doing the extra climb, I recommend you turn right to walk down the seam and follow it directly to the river. The old creek bed, which will be dry in the summer, provides easy walking without the extra hill climb to reach the river.

Environment and Fish

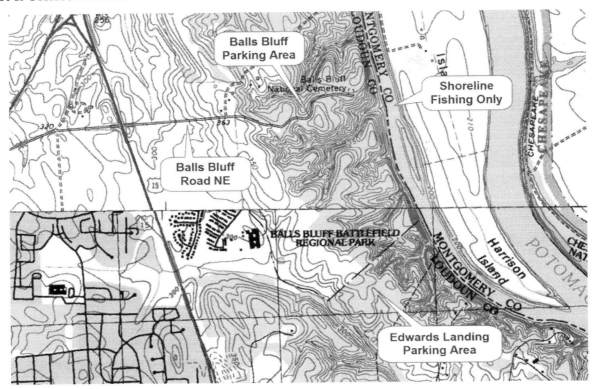

Balls Bluff Battlefield

The layout of Balls Bluff is almost identical to the Red Rock Wilderness with the exception that it lacks the same extent of wide, open parkland paralleling the river. However, the trail winding through the trees along the shoreline is easy to negotiate and is not obstructed by logs or brush. This is a good place to fish on a hot day as a result of the thick shade that protects both the riverbank and the deep, muddy channel that runs next to it.

The current is lazy. With nothing to push the silt downstream, vegetation covers the river bottom in late summer. Luckily, the shoreline is deep enough to prevent vegetation from growing since this is the only area you can fish. The bass collect there, huddled under the fallen logs, and enjoy the coolness out of the sun.
As a result of the tree cover, you will be frustrated if you try and fish using fly gear. This is another place where the only correct tool is a spin rod. If you fish directly up and downstream, you might get a few halting casts out, but will spend most of the time untangling your fly from trees either in front or in back of you. It's a shame, because this is an ideal place to flip small poppers next to the still water around the

fallen structure. You can still do that with larger poppers or other top water presentations using your spin gear.

Given that this is a side channel, the mud is not washed downstream as thoroughly as it is in the main river. There are a few places where the river appears shallow and you might be tempted to wade. You will discover the folly of this strategy as you sink a foot or more into the soft muck that lines the river's edge. On the other hand, there are plenty of good spots where you can stand and fish directly from the shore without getting wet.

This section of the river is best fished from a boat. If you float down the side channel, you can fish both sides as well as identify and target some of the rock structure that occurs where the current moves a little faster and pushes the mud downstream. The area directly below the cemetery is good.

This is the view upstream from where the red trail hits the river at 39.129111,-77.52511

The thick cover shown in the picture is normal and persists along the entire riverbank.

The downstream picture is almost identical.

I have not discovered a good spot to wade away from the bank. There probably is one someplace on this stretch. If you find it, you will have discovered a real treasure as it will allow you to target the shoreline at the edge of the overhanging branches.

The Point of Rocks gage was running at 1.12 ft in this picture and the Little Falls gage was 2.81 ft.

Fallen trees collect into large tangles to form perfect habitat in many places.

Edwards Landing

Edwards landing presents the same basic challenge as Balls Bluff. The shoreline is pitched and deep; prohibiting wading. Frankly, I have not fully investigated this particular access point and if you move up or downstream, you may find a place or two where you can get into the river. Be aware that private property starts directly downstream of this Park, so focus your efforts moving upstream.

This is the view looking upstream from 39.123102,-77.522106.

The shore is identical to what you encounter in Balls Bluff with dense trees overhanging the river preventing easy casting.

The view downstream shows even more obstacles as the Park ends and private property begins.

Bottom line

Unless I'm in a boat, I'm not interested in fishing this particular location. The forest that runs all the way to the shoreline restricts the ability to fish. On the other hand, not many people fish here, so it is relatively unpressured when compared to the more popular areas of the river. If you live close by and only have an hour or two to fish, this may be a good place for you to come.

Whites Ferry

Google Map Coordinates: 39.154524,-77.519403

Summary Rating

Pressure	Red	Canoe/Kayak Launch	Green
Physical Fitness	Green	Trailer Boat Launch	Green
Wading	Yellow	Parking	Green
Shore Fishing	Yellow	Regulations	Green
Spin Fishing	Green	Fly Fishing	Green
Scenery	Yellow	Overall	Yellow

Special Regulations

Maryland enforces a catch and release regulation for all bass between Seneca Breaks and the mouth of the Monocacy River.

Getting to the Stream

Virginia: From Leesburg, go north on US 15 and make a right turn on Whites Ferry Road (SR 655). Follow it to the ferry and take the ferry across the river. Nominally, the ferry runs every 20 minutes.

Maryland: From I-270, take the exit for MD 28W. stay on MD 28 for approximately 12 miles until it splits north at Darnestown. Take the left fork in Darnestown on Whites Ferry Road (MD 107) and follow it to the river.

There is a parking lot near the store. You have to pay a fee to launch a boat. You can do that inside the store and pick up snacks at the same time. There are numerous trails that lead to the river on either side of the ferry landing. During the summer, a substantial backup of traffic can occur. If you intend to use the ferry, leave yourself plenty of time.

Unfortunately, the land on the Virginia shoreline is privately owned and heavily posted. Given that the road runs right next to the shoreline, you might wonder if the landowner is posting an area that is subject to the VDOT easement. I had the same question and checked the County records to determine the property line. There is a plenty of room between the road and the river beyond the easement. Therefore, the landowner has the right to post this property. This is a shame since some of the best wading in this area is near the corner where Whites Ferry Road turns north to run in parallel with the river as it approaches the ferry ramp (39.147901,-77.524467). You'll need a boat to get access to that prime spot.

This is the Maryland Landing of the ferry.

Note the forested banks.

There are picnic areas on either side of the road and the small store sells basic supplies for fishing.

Environment and Fish

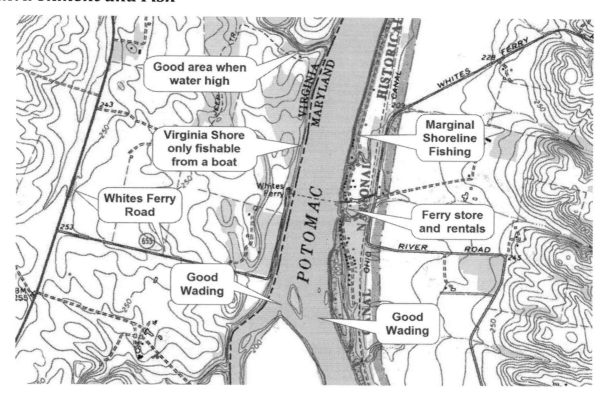

Whites Ferry is one of the best fishing locations between Seneca Breaks and Harpers Ferry... if you have a boat. The rest of us have to make do with other options. The character of the river is dramatically different depending on whether you point your rod upstream or down.

The Maryland shoreline upriver from the ferry, while open, terminates in a wide, muddy shelf that quickly drops off to an unwadeable depth. During the summer, thick vegetation grows in this area and makes for hard fishing. You can fish from the Maryland shoreline if you content yourself with catching sunfish. The habitat within casting distance of the shore is marginal and doesn't get much better if you wade out the 10 to 20 feet allowed by the shallow shelf. If the Maryland side above the ferry represents the absolute worst bass water you can imagine, the Virginia side is the exact opposite.

The main current of the river spins downstream along the northern shore of Mason Island at the far bend. The entire volume, pushed at high velocity in the spring, slams against the Virginia shore and scours it clean. This leaves the perfect habitat for smallmouth bass. It's full of rocks and boulders with the minimum of mud and sand. On any given summer day, a parade of boats drifts downstream; fishing the steep bank and cliff face between Mason Island and the ferry. If you have a boat, don't forget to fish Limestone Branch where it joins the Potomac.

You do not have the opportunity to access the Virginia shoreline on foot. It's all private property and it's too deep to wade up from the ferry.

Downstream from the ferry on the Maryland shore, the opportunities to wade improve. Walk down the towpath for a half mile, cut over to the river and wade across the backwater to get to the shore opposite the tip of Harrison Island. There is some good structure here that runs all the way across the river. You may not be able to move all the way to Virginia as a result of the scattered deep areas.

If you are going to fish from the shoreline, bring your spin rod as the banks are thick with trees and underbrush. Fly anglers can use their gear if they can get out far enough away from the shore to deploy an effective backcast.

The river is featureless and frustrating to fish from the Maryland shoreline given the poor bass structure on that side.

It is impossible to fish from the Virginia shoreline as a result of private property.

The Maryland shoreline upstream (on the right), while easily accessible, overlooks a non-productive section of the river.

The river at the corner of Whites Ferry Road near the tip of Harrison Island (left side of picture) is all wadeable.

The Potomac is wadeable on both sides of the tip of Harrison island.

The Virginia shoreline is all posted private property.

The chute at the tip of Harrison Island is wadeable and productive.

This picture was taken from the Virginia side.

The Point of Rocks gage was running at 1.09 ft (very low) on the day this picture was taken and the Little Falls gage was 2.72 ft.

Bottom line

There's a little bit of everything at Whites Ferry. If you are willing to walk downstream from the ferry, you can move into water between Maryland and Harrison Island where it is shallow enough to allow wading. The best way to fish this section is from a kayak or canoe. After launching from Whites Ferry, paddle over to the Virginia shore and fish the chute between the islands, then head upstream and fish the superlative structure along the Virginia bank and end the day in the narrow area between Harrison Island and Maryland where you can pop out of your boat and wade again.

Dickerson State Conservation Park

Google Map Coordinates: 39.19483,-77.469363

Summary Rating

Pressure	**Green**	Canoe/Kayak Launch	**Red**
Physical Fitness	**Yellow**	Trailer Boat Launch	**Red**
Wading	**Green**	Parking	**Green**
Shore Fishing	**Green**	Regulations	**Green**
Spin Fishing	**Green**	Fly Fishing	**Green**
Scenery	**Yellow**	Overall	**Green**

Special Regulations

Maryland enforces a catch and release regulation for all bass between Seneca Breaks and the mouth of the Monocacy River.

Getting to the Stream

Virginia: To get to Maryland, you can either take Whites Ferry across the river or drive up to Point of Rocks. Given the extensive backups that occur at the ferry in the summer, I recommend you drive the extra distance. Take US 15 north from Leesburg and cross the river at Point of Rocks. Take an immediate right turn on MD 28 (Clay Street) and follow it through some turns for over nine miles. Turn right on Martinsburg Road and follow it for 1.6 miles.

Maryland: From I-270, take the exit for MD 109 (Old Hundred Road) and follow it to Beallsville where you turn right on MD 28. MD 28 dead ends into Martinsburg Road. Turn left and follow it for 1.6 miles.

There is a sharp right turn at 39.195046,-77.46490 that leads to the parking area.

Once you reach the parking area, follow the path past the kiosk at the south end of the parking lot. Do not walk onto the towpath! Instead, look for the wide path that leads down a small hill into a gully where the path from the kiosk joins the towpath. Follow the trail to the river.

Go through the gate and continue on the path.

I was disoriented the first time I was here and wandered down the towpath for a half mile before I realized I was not getting closer to the river.

Once you are through the gully, the path becomes better defined.

Environment and Fish

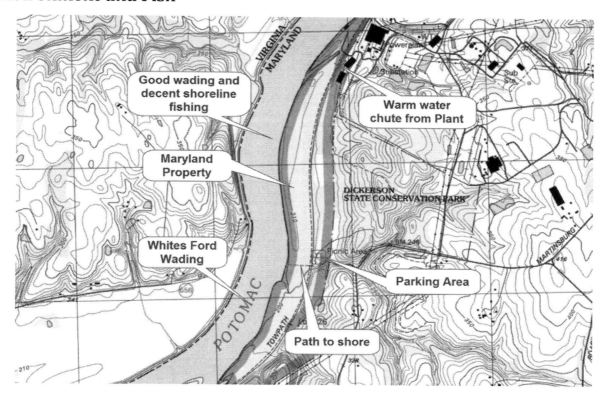

Included in the 304 acre Dickerson Conservation Park is the grand attraction of fishing downstream in the warm water discharge from the Dickerson Power Plant. If you need a good place to fish for smallmouth bass in the heart of winter, this is your spot. With the water churning out of the plant at a toasty 65°, it creates a two-mile long warm water plume that attracts the attention of fish struggling with the cold of winter. The extra squirt of warmth keeps the fish active longer. The colder it gets, the closer you should fish to the power plant to maximize the advantage of the warm water since it cools quickly when it mixes with the frigid water rolling south from West Virginia.

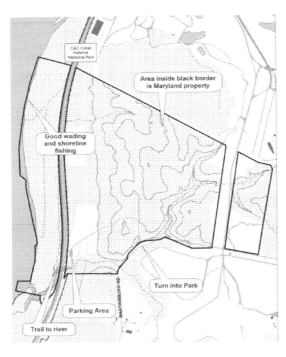

The entire shoreline south of the power plant is fishable since it features a gentle shelf that stretches for a good distance into the river. While there are deep pockets here and there, wading is easy and the fish cooperate.

Shoreline fishing is good in the deeper spots. Even when the weather gets cold, there are plenty of fish that cruise the shallows in pursuit of bait fish.

While many regard Dickerson has a winter fishing location, those who do will lose out on the opportunity to fish the shallow water in the vicinity of Whites Ford (39.190988,-77.473183); a half mile south.

Whites Ford is easy to wade in the summer with productive riffle beds on the downstream side of the rocks until the temperature gets too high from the combination of normal summer heat and the discharge.

There is no problem using either fly or spin gear in this location. Fly anglers have an advantage given the shallow nature of most of the shelf and is one place where they can dispense with the sinking tip. However, the fish hold next to the bottom so be sure you get your fly or your lure down to where they will see it.

The perspective looking upstream from 39.19439, -77.47161.

The shoreline is broad, gently sloping and open with easy wading into the river.

Looking downstream from the same place.

The Point of Rocks gage was running at 1.68 ft when this picture was taken and the Little Falls gage was 3.28 ft.

Bottom line

This is the perfect place for cold weather fishing. I have read reports of other anglers having hundred plus fish days in January or February downstream of the warm water discharge. While I have not gone to "fish heaven" here as they must have done, this is a solid place to spend the day. When you get the itch to fish in the middle of the winter or early spring, a visit to the Dickerson Conservation Park can calm you down and give you jolt you need to survive until the fishing season roars back later in the year.

Monocacy River Launch

Google Map Coordinates: 39.224607,-77.44945

Summary Rating

Pressure	**Yellow**	Canoe/Kayak Launch	**Green**
Physical Fitness	**Green**	Trailer Boat Launch	**Green**
Wading	**Yellow**	Parking	**Green**
Shore Fishing	**Yellow**	Regulations	**Yellow**
Spin Fishing	**Green**	Fly Fishing	**Green**
Scenery	**Yellow**	Overall	**Green**

Special Regulations

Maryland enforces a catch and release regulation for all bass between Seneca Breaks and the mouth of the Monocacy River. You can keep fish upstream of the river's mouth. I strongly encourage you to continue to catch and release wherever you are on the Potomac.

If you plan to actually fish in the Monocacy River, it is not covered by the reciprocal agreement with Virginia. You need a Maryland license.

There are no federal restrictions on entering the river between here and Harpers Ferry.

Getting to the Stream

Virginia: Take US 15 north from Leesburg and cross the river at Point of Rocks. Take an immediate right turn on MD 28 (Clay Street) and follow it through some turns for 8 miles. Turn right at Mouth of Monocacy Road and follow it to the park.

Maryland: Take exit 22 from I-270 and head west on MD 109 (Old Hundred Road). Turn right on Barnesville Road. Turn left on MD 95 (Mt Ephraim Road). Turn right on Monocacy Road and follow it to the park.

Once in the park, take the right fork to get to the boat launch or the left fork to go to the parking area near the towpath. There are picnic facilities and a public restroom available.

The boat launch is actually on the Monocacy River and the Potomac is approximately 1,000 feet downstream to the left. If you start your day in a canoe or kayak, paddle underneath the towpath to reach the river. Using a boat allows you to move across the river and reach the Virginia shoreline that is wadeable at low levels. If you do not have a boat and want to wade, hop on the towpath and walk across the aqueduct to move north along the Maryland shoreline. Your destination is Cox Island. No need for shore fishers to walk anywhere. They can start fishing at the junction of the two rivers.

The towpath runs across this historic aqueduct (39.223892,-77.452165).

The best fishing for waders is along the Maryland shoreline near Cox island.

You can fish from the shore downstream from the parking area.

Environment and Fish

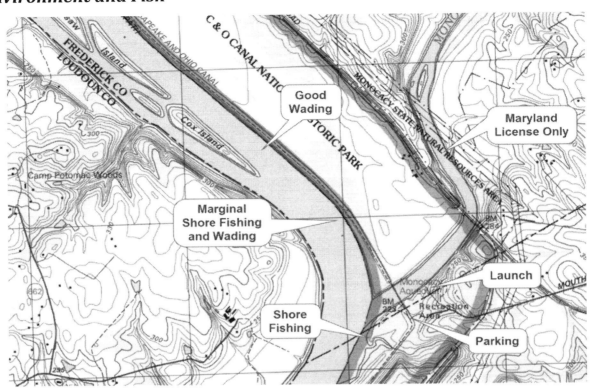

First, don't bother to fish the Monocacy River. The bottom is uniformly muddy, featureless and is not worth the time with great fishing on the Potomac a few yards downstream.

The best option for wading is to walk upriver along the towpath until you get adjacent to Cox Island (39.233126,-77.466091). While there are other opportunities to wade along the Maryland shoreline before you get to the island, the river shallows out significantly near Cox Island and permits you to get away from the shore. The area near Cox Island includes the required deep channels that hold smallmouth bass. Prior to reaching Cox Island, you may find a few places where you can wade out on the narrow shelf that extends a short distance into the river from the Maryland shoreline. There is a similar, but broader shelf, on the Virginia shore.

The Maryland shelf terminates on a trench that has deep holes that can go 8 feet or greater -- making the need to wear a PFD in this area compelling. The bottom of the river is a mix of sand, large rocks, and gravel with a few large boulders providing good targets

To reach the start of the good wading area, walk approximately 0.8 miles along the towpath. At that point (39.23237, -77.46063), cut over to the river and begin fishing upstream. Once you enter the river, you can move at will in the area around Cox Island. As you fish out into the middle of the river, the shelf breaks off into a deeper trench (5 feet) that holds a good population of smallmouth bass. Once you fish the trench, work around it on the upstream side and continue to fish in any direction. There are large boulders underneath the water and each is a potential honey hole.

While you may be tempted to walk across Cox Island and fish the other side, I don't recommend it because the side channel to the west of Cox Island is out of the main flow of the river and tends to become extremely shallow; worsening the farther upstream you walk.

The story for shoreline fishers is not as positive. While they can fish downstream from the parking lot for a decent distance, moving in the opposite direction presents a significant challenge. Walking up the shoreline is problematic depending on the water levels and you may have to wade in the mud that collects near the bank if you do not want to bushwhack back and forth from the towpath.

From a fishing technique perspective, either fly or spin gear will work just fine. If you use a fly rod, be sure and put on an intermediate sinking tip when you target the center of the river. Obviously, remove that if you deploy poppers or dry flies near the shoreline. From a spin perspective, the lure of choice in this area, confirmed by many conversations with fellow anglers at the boat launch, is a three or four inch long grub.

This is the view downstream from the mouth of the river towards the Dickerson Power Plant (39.208581,-77.46563).

The best access for shore anglers is downstream along the Maryland bank. The vegetation hangs back a little bit from the river and tolerates your presence. It eventually closes out and becomes thick.

This is the shoreline looking upstream in the vicinity of Cox Island.

Note the thick, overhanging vegetation on the Maryland shore at the right. This restricts access to a few open spaces where you can bushwhack to and from the towpath. Waders can move out into the river and fish up and down at will near Cox Island.

The Point of Rocks gage was 1.45 ft when this picture was taken -- an ideal level for wading.

Bottom line

If you are willing to walk a short distance on the towpath, you will be rewarded with good wading. Shore anglers are limited to the easy area near the junction of the Monocacy and the Potomac.

Nolands Ferry

Google Map Coordinates: 39.249869,-77.482367

Summary Rating

Pressure	Yellow	Canoe/Kayak Launch	Green
Physical Fitness	Green	Trailer Boat Launch	Green
Wading	Yellow	Parking	Green
Shore Fishing	Red	Regulations	Yellow
Spin Fishing	Green	Fly Fishing	Green
Scenery	Yellow	Overall	Yellow

Special Regulations

None.

Getting to the Stream

Virginia: Take US 15 north from Leesburg and cross the river at Point of Rocks. Take an immediate right turn on Clay Street and drive 4 miles. Turn right on New Design Road and follow it to the launch area.

Maryland: From Frederick, go South on I-270 and take exit 31B onto MD 85 towards Buckeytown. Stay on MD 85 for almost 9 miles and turn right on MD 28W (Tuscarora Road). Turn right on Nolands Ferry Road with another right on New Design Road.

If you intend to drop a trailered boat in the water using this launch, be careful on the steep launch ramp if conditions are slick.

Environment and Fish

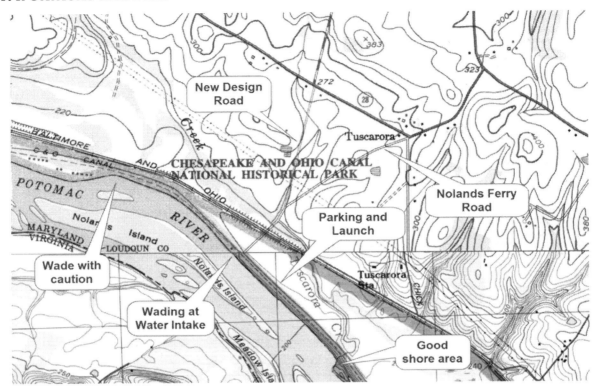

This area continues the sad trend for shoreline fishers set downstream at the Monocacy River junction. As horrible as wading access was at Red Rocks and Balls Bluff, shore fishers experience a comparable horror in this location. The Maryland shoreline continues to be packed with dense vegetation and trees that cluster on a high, steep river bank. While shore fishers can scramble down to the river in specific places, it will be a very physical day of bushwhacking back and forth to the towpath. The one ideal place to fish from the shore is at the junction of Tuscarora Creek (39.24358, -77.47552); a quick 0.6 mile walk down from the parking area. This is a good location for catfish in addition to bass.

If you're willing to wade, you have more options. While, at good water levels, you can start fishing up or downstream from the launch area, I recommend you walk 0.65 miles west on the towpath to 39.255103,-77.492162 and cut south to the river from there. There is a hump in the river in this location that forms two small islands and creates channels. Fish the islands paying special attention to the chutes as well as the downstream tips. The current can be strong, so be careful.

Once you finish, fish downstream on the narrow shelf that extends out from the Maryland shore. You will have to get in and out of the river depending on the water levels as there are some deep holes near the bank. The County water intake (39.250336,-77.483839) borders shallow water and is another good area for wading. Obviously, stay away from the concrete structure itself.

Below the boat launch, walk down to the intersection of Tuscarora Creek and move out on the small island that hangs at the mouth of the creek. Fish around and out from the island.

You can use both fly and spin gear effectively here. Fly fishers have the additional advantage of being able to work small poppers along the shaded shoreline.

The shoreline bordering Nolands is packed with overhanging trees and vegetation that makes shoreline fishing an exercise in frustration.

It's frustrating not in the sense of limited casting with spin gear, but that your movement is constrained and awkward.

You can wade near the County water intake structure shown at the far right in this picture.

The shallow shelf near the intake extends up and downstream.

The Point of Rocks gage was high at 2.54 ft on the day this picture was taken, but it was still shallow enough to wade into the river at that spot.

Bottom line

Nolands Landing offers some wading access for a significant distance along the river and is a good alternative if Point of Rocks is too crowded. It's a bad place for shore fishing.

Point of Rocks

Google Map Coordinates: 39.271942, -77.547054

Summary Rating

Pressure	Red	Canoe/Kayak Launch	Green
Physical Fitness	Green	Trailer Boat Launch	Green
Wading	Yellow	Parking	Green
Shore Fishing	Yellow	Regulations	Yellow
Spin Fishing	Green	Fly Fishing	Green
Scenery	Green	Overall	Green

Special Regulations

None.

Getting to the Stream

Virginia Side: Follow Rt 15 either north from Virginia or south from Maryland towards the river. Turn north on Lovettsville road on the Virginia side of the bridge. Take an immediate right on the dirt road.

Maryland Side: Turn east onto Clay Street from Rt 15 near the bridge. Take an immediate right onto Commerce Street and follow it to the right hand turn leading across the railroad tracks. Follow the road to the parking area near the bridge.

On the Virginia side, private property borders both sides of the boat launch. A well beaten and well used trail leads north along the shore upstream from the Virginia boat launch, but it is posted and you should not trespass even though you will see plenty of other people doing just that. All of the property on the Maryland side is within the C&O Canal NHP.

Maryland has the best facilities for picnicking and other activities unrelated to fishing.

The large parking area overlooks a broad grassy plain that is perfect for family activities.

The river is deep enough next to the shoreline to allow fishing but also has a ridge 200 feet below the launch for those who prefer to wade.

Environment and Fish

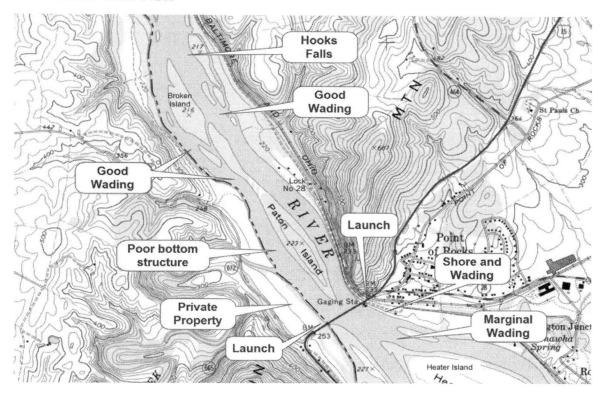

You will have a totally different day depending on whether you stay on the Virginia or Maryland side of Paton Island. This key landmark splits the river just upstream of the bridge.

Virginia

While you can wade directly out from the boat launch and fish the tip of the island as well as the area underneath the bridge, the best fishing on the Virginia side is approximately a mile upstream near the chute between Broken Island and Paton Island (39.28118,-77.553402). At that point, there is a series of rapids where the river pushes down the Virginia side of Broken Island to form some nice pools interspersed with boulders and other rock structure. The problem is getting to this place legally. While the path on the shoreline extends the entire distance up to this point, it is on private property and well marked with "posted" signs. The legal way to obtain access is to wade out into the river and walk up the center. At normal flows in the middle of summer, the water isn't deep and, although it represents a tough physical challenge to walk a mile in the river, it will be worth it.

En route to the riffles, spend some time fishing where Catoctin Creek merges with the river from the south. There is an uncommonly deep pool at this location that is well worth your attention. As you walk and fish your way up towards the rapids, you can target the deeper channels but I recommend you not waste much time on them since the river runs over a sandy bottom that is not attractive to smallmouth. You can certainly catch as many sunfish in this area as you care to pull in.

Once you reach the gradient break marked by the rapids that stretch between the shoreline and the chute, spend a good deal of time on the section immediately downstream. The water deepens the farther you move away from the Virginia shore and the drop-off can be very productive. Cast as far as you can towards the island to reach the deeper water. You can pick up some good smallmouth bass in the highly oxygenated water directly below this first gradient break. If you have a canoe, the deepest spot in this stretch is just below the chute near Paton Island. It holds massive catfish and equally large smallmouth bass. Move upstream to continue to fish on the Virginia side of Broken Island. It is easy wading all the way up to the northern point of Broken Island and you can spend the entire day in this thousand foot stretch. Given that the only way most people fish here is to canoe downriver from Lander, the pressure is minimal and, other than the folks floating through on canoes and kayaks who typically move quickly using "float by" fishing techniques, you will have this section of the river to yourself.

Moving south from the Virginia launch, the opportunities for wading are not as good. There is a shallow shelf that exists underneath the bridge and you can use this to move out into the river to fish some of the ridges that trace perpendicular to the shoreline. The water deepens the farther you go downstream and limits wading to the shoreline area -- eventually closing you out. On a typical Saturday afternoon, this particular location is clogged with huge numbers of picnickers who take the opportunity to play in the river.

Unless you are willing to get your feet wet, there is no real shoreline fishing opportunity on the Virginia side given the issues associated with private property on either side.

Both fly and spin fishers will have a field day in this location.

This is the view upstream from the tip of Paton Island (39.273519,-77.5463).

The entire river is wadeable at normal water levels.

The Point of Rocks gage was running at 2.01 ft when this picture was taken.

This picture looks back towards the Virginia launch.

The entire broad section between the launch and the island is shallow and easy to wade at normal levels.

As you would expect, the river in the immediate vicinity of the launch is highly pressured by casual anglers.

This is the channel down the Virginia side with Heater Island on the left.

When the water level at the Point of Rocks gage is at 1.4 ft or below, you can wade from Maryland to the island if you pick your path carefully.

The water level when this picture was taken was 1.23 ft.

Maryland

Do not try and enter the river by wading in at the boat launch itself. There's a deep hole at the end of the ramp.

The Maryland branch is the stark opposite of the Virginia side. The main force of the river moves down this channel and it keeps the bottom clean of the silt and sand that create the featureless, barren river bottom on the Virginia side. If you need proof, just sit for a bit and count the number of bass boats fishing down the Maryland side versus Virginia. It's no contest.

Upstream

Other than the ledge that reaches into the river approximately 200 feet below the bridge, wading anglers must walk to reach the best water. Shoreline fishers, on the other hand, can start fishing directly in the deep hole underneath the bridge and then down to hit the water above and below the ledge.

Shore fishers who move up the towpath will have to select entry and exit points because there is no easy passage along the shoreline. They will spend the day moving back and forth to the towpath as they switch fishing locations. At least the towpath is within spitting distance of the river; making the transitions as painless as possible.

Waders must walk up the towpath and locate the individual rock ridges that start at the bank and move out into the main body. For those who do, there is productive fishing in the pools above and below those ridge structures. Your first opportunity occurs at 39.279661,-77.546713 where the towpath veers away from the river, but even this spot can be deep at times.

The best place to go is to walk just over 1.25 miles to 39.287313,-77.552834 and cut over to the river from there. This opens up on a rocky section (39.285785,-77.555108) that is upstream of the chute between Paton and Broken Islands. If you have the energy, continue up the river on the towpath to fish Hooks Falls from the shore at 39.289804,-77.558466. To reach this area from the towpath, you have to wade across a small backwater followed by a narrow island. A better strategy, if the water level cooperates, is to stay in the river where the towpath veered away and walk up the shoreline since there is plenty of structure to fish as you work your way north. If you were thinking about buying a bike to support your fishing activities, this location is the perfect place to leverage that rapid means of transportation.

Downstream

Shore fishers can fish downstream from the bridge for as far as they want to fight the shoreline vegetation that starts downstream of the grassy area. For those who want to wade, there is a rock ledge that extends from the upper part of the grassy area out into the center of the river. It is only accessible when the water level is low, but if you can get on it, you can fish the deep pool that lies just downstream. In addition, you can strap on your PFD and wade to the small island just downstream of the parking area. From the tip of that island, you can work your way across to Heater Island. Once you get over to Heater Island, fish the grass that grows in the vicinity of the tip as well as fish down the shoreline to the small high spot that appears in the vicinity of 39.270728,-77.539541.

You can use either fly or spin gear in this stretch productively. Fly fishers will have a great time using top water presentations against all of the rock structure. Spin fishers need to be careful of getting hung up on the rocks when fishing the ledges and I recommend they use Texas rigged or other similar weedless presentations.

This is the view up the river from the Maryland side of Paton Island.

Note the congested vegetation on the shoreline to the right of the picture.

The trees and bushes hang off the steep bank supporting the towpath. There is no room at water level along the shoreline to move up or downstream.

This is the narrow channel on the Maryland side that leads from the small island that separates Heater Island from the shore.

If you choose your way carefully, you can work across this channel when the water level is running at 1.4 ft or less.

The Point of Rocks gage was 1.25 ft when this picture was taken.

Bottom line

I recommend Point of Rocks. I know it's busy given the density of cars in the parking lot and the throngs of people near the bridge. However, they do not venture very far into the river and you will not find anybody else fishing away from the launch areas other than individuals who have boats. Bring a bike and work the Maryland side!

Lander

Google Map Coordinates: 39.305193,-77.560424

Summary Rating

Pressure	Red	Canoe/Kayak Launch	Green
Physical Fitness	Green	Trailer Boat Launch	Green
Wading	Green	Parking	Green
Shore Fishing	Green	Regulations	Yellow
Spin Fishing	Green	Fly Fishing	Green
Scenery	Green	Overall	Green

Special Regulations

None.

Getting to the Stream

South: Follow US 15 north out of Leesburg. Cross the river and take the first left after the bridge onto Point of Rocks Road (MD 464).

North: Follow US 15 south from US 340. Turn right onto Point of Rocks Road (MD 464) approximately a mile north of the bridge.

Follow Point of Rocks Road for 1.4 miles and turn left on Lander Road. Cross the railroad tracks at the bottom of the hill and follow the road to the left to get to the launch.

Environment and Fish

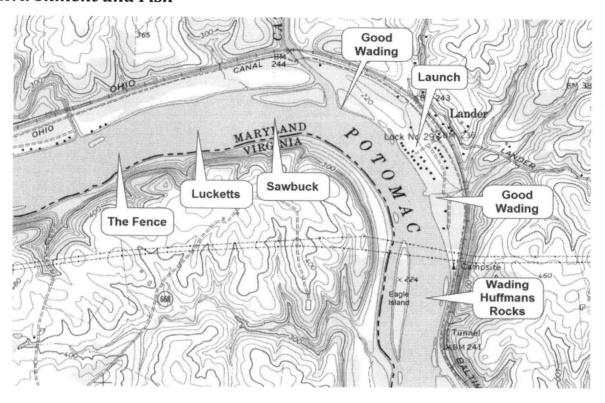

Lander is one of the most popular places on the river for anglers. Most of the folks who use this facility launch trailered boats and move upstream to fish the fast water near rapids named Sawbuck, Lucketts Ferry or the Fence. Downstream, they target the unique parallel ridge structure near Eagle Island called Huffmans Rocks; moving from there down the Maryland side of the river to the Point of Rocks. In fact, Point of Rocks is only 2.5 miles downstream from Lander if you take the towpath. For those of you who have a canoe and a bike, you may want to lock your bike next to a tree at Point of Rocks, go back to Lander, launch your canoe, fish back to Point of Rocks and use the bike to shuttle back to your vehicle while your fishing buddy watches your gear and continues to fish around the bridge.

The dilemma at Lander will be "go upstream or down?" Either choice is a good option. If you go upstream, you can begin fishing right away and work your way all the way up to the junction where Catoctin Creek joins the river from the north. The area immediately around the launch ramp is a little deep so you need to move upstream to where the shallow shelf begins. It extends about 20 yards out into the main current. Fish your way up to the junction of the creek and work out on the ledge that forms at the tip of Little Catoctin Island. If the water level is right, don't ignore fishing the creek itself. From there, you can continue up the river to fish the downstream edge of the Sawbuck rapid that marks the upper boundary of the island. The area immediately upstream of Sawbuck gets grassy in late summer and is too deep to wade. If you do not mind walking, there is wading upstream of the Lucketts Ferry Rapids at 39.308269,-77.57515 at low water.

Moving south from the boat launch, the shallow water continues down to the power lines that stretch across the river at 39.299618,-77.558026. However, it is not absolutely reliable that you will be able to wade in this section. The full force of the current hits this bank and unless the conditions are perfect, you may find it too deep. If that's the case, continue downstream to the Eagle Island campground at mile marker 50.3 on the towpath.

When you look out from the Eagle Island campground, you're looking at a long ridge structure running parallel with the direction of flow called Huffmans Rocks. You can wade in this area although it can be deep at times. You have to pick your track carefully and may find yourself confined to the narrow shelf along the shoreline.

Shoreline fishers will have problems once they move outside of the area of the boat launch. Like the rest of the river, the banks remain reasonably steep, are full of vegetation and present significant obstacles limiting access to the shoreline. There is no defined edge at the base of the towpath that allows you to walk down the shoreline. The trees are large and overhang the river; creating a wall of branches and leaves that restricts your ability to cast. If you're going to fish from the shore in this area, I recommend you move upstream since the bank is more open in that direction.

Both fly and spin fishers can use their equipment to good advantage. Fly fishers should rig up with an intermediate sink tip to ensure they can work the bottom. Downstream from Bald Eagle Island campground, you can fish your way down the narrow shelf that extends from the shore and target the overhanging vegetation with poppers. Spin fishers can do the same; leveraging smaller grubs rigged weedless. I recommend the three inch grub with my personal favorite color for this area being the powerbait "Christmas Lights." Tubes are always good.

This is the view looking upstream from the boat launch when the water was at the upper threshold of the wading.

The Point of Rocks gage was 1.68 ft when this picture was taken.

This is the downstream perspective from the boat launch. You can see the tip of the Bald Eagle Island (39.29726,-77.561095) in the distance to the right of the boat.

Huffmans Rocks lie in the channel to the left of the island.

This is the view of Huffmans Rocks looking downstream from 39.29531,-77.55786.

The Point of Rocks gage was 1.68 ft when this picture was taken.

If you have a canoe to get across the river, be sure to fish the willow grass that grows on the eastern shoreline at the upper end of Bald Eagle Island (39.300457,-77.560741).

If you do that, don't bother to fish down the west side of the island since the water is shallow with minimal current. You can catch plenty of sunfish, but the bass are not interested in hanging out there.

Another view of Huffmans Rocks from a different vantage point at 39.29628,-77.55779.

There is a shallow shelf that extends out into the river from this location.

Bottom line

Lander's popularity is justified. While those who can get out on the river in a boat will have an advantage, there are plenty of places where moving slowly along the shoreline will yield plenty of fish.

Brunswick Campground

Google Map Coordinates: 39.304118,-77.596178

Summary Rating

Pressure	**Green**	Canoe/Kayak Launch	**Green**
Physical Fitness	**Green**	Trailer Boat Launch	**Green**
Wading	**Green**	Parking	**Green**
Shore Fishing	**Red**	Regulations	**Yellow**
Spin Fishing	**Green**	Fly Fishing	**Green**
Scenery	**Yellow**	Overall	**Green**

Special Regulations

None.

Getting to the Stream

From Virginia: Northbound on Rt 17 from Virginia, cross the river and continue to the traffic circle in Brunswick. Take the second exit from the circle onto East A Street.

From Maryland: From US 340 going west from Frederick, turn south on Rt 17 at the Burkittsville exit. At the traffic circle that marks the junction with Rt 180, take the second exit to stay on Rt 17 and follow that into town. At the traffic circle in town, take the fourth exit onto East A Street.

Turn right on North Maple Ave and follow it across the train tracks. When it dead ends on a dirt road, turn left and follow it to the campground.

The Brunswick Campground is a hidden asset located on the southern fringe of the small town of Brunswick, Maryland. It boasts 65 recreational vehicle and 310 tent sites complete with pavilions, picnic tables, 30 amp electrical service and water hookups. During the summer of 2009, they offered free wireless Internet within a reasonable distance of the Campground office. All that is good news for those who need an inexpensive place to stay while exploiting the superb fishing between Brunswick and Harpers Ferry. The Campground opens the first weekend in April and closes the last weekend in November, so it is in operation during the entire "prime time" fishing season. For those who want to launch a canoe or a trailered boat, there is a concrete boat launch and, just like the launch in the center of town, there is no fee to use it.

The Campground is perched at the edge of the towpath. Even if you do not camp here, you can park in the lot to the left of the entrance and move directly to the towpath to leverage it as a high speed route for points east. This is an ideal place to use a bike to move from location to location so you spend more time in the water instead of pounding shoe leather.

Environment and Fish

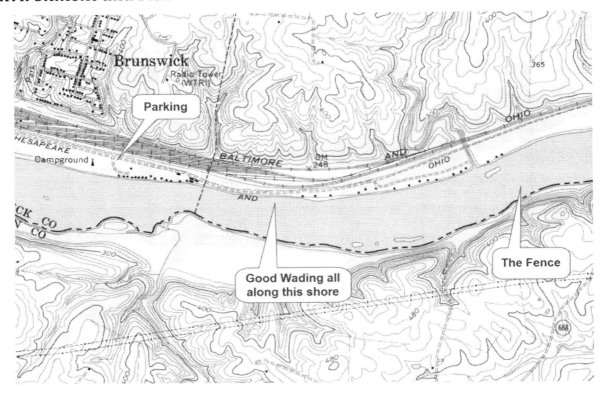

While you can wade upstream, my preference is to walk down the towpath and fish downstream towards Lander. Once you leave the Campground, continue on the towpath for approximately a half-mile to 39.305803,-77.605298. This is where the towpath veers back towards the river and, depending on the amount of vegetation on the trees; you get a good first look at the river here.

If you decide not to hop into the river, the towpath begins to run on top of a very steep bank that makes it difficult to reach the river's edge without picking your spots carefully. At any rate, you want to start fishing at this location since there is a small gradient break that produces a one hundred yard stretch of riffled water. Fish downstream and pay attention to the heavily vegetated shoreline that is replete with fallen timber and other good fish-holding structure.

Once you enter the river, the steep bank restricts your ability to exit unless you are part mountain goat. For the next 0.4 miles, remain in the river until you get to 39.304351,-77.597487 where a small peninsula sticks out. At this point, there is a gentle slope leading from the river's edge back to the towpath that makes for an easy, un-stressful exit with the minimum amount of bushwhacking. This is only 0.4 miles downstream from where you started and can fill a good afternoon. Before you leave the river, be sure to fish out from the peninsula where there are good boulders sheltering deeper channels.

In addition to fishing the shoreline while wading, you can wander out into the main stream of the river. At a level of 1.5 feet at the Point of Rocks gage, there are high spots and ridges tracking to the center of the river. Wade along these to fish some of the deeper holes and runs scattered throughout this area. If you do decide to move away from the shoreline, and are not wearing a PFD, I recommend you reverse that decision. There are deep spots and you could find yourself floating downstream if you're not careful.

The main current of the river favors the center and Virginia side with kayakers and canoeists leveraging the higher velocity to move downstream.

If you have plenty of energy, you can go all the way down to 39.306082,-77.584419. This spot is approximately 1.6 miles away from the Campground. Fish the good structure, called "The Fence", and then work your way back upstream towards the Campground. Don't bother to go farther east than the Fence because, at that point, you're closer to the Lander access point and should use it to fish farther downriver.

Looking upstream from where the towpath rejoins the river at 39.304666,-77.602165.

Downstream from here, the bank gets steep.

The river offers a sweeping panorama that camouflages the shallow nature of this section.

Downstream from the same location.

The water was running at 1.07 ft at the Point of Rocks gage on the day this picture was taken. That number is very close to the low point.

At higher levels, you will not be able to wade as far out into the center of the river.

Bottom line

While this part of the river does not offer spectacular scenery with dramatic, craggy rocks scattered across the broad expanse of the river, it's nothing but good. The bottom is rocky with plenty of undersurface structure that makes this a haven for smallmouth bass. The wading is easy since you do not have to contend with varying velocities of water created by breaks in the ridge structure. Instead, the push is constant and predictable.

Brunswick Launch

Google Map Coordinates: 39.311025,-77.630682

Summary Rating

Pressure	Yellow	Canoe/Kayak Launch	Green
Physical Fitness	Yellow	Trailer Boat Launch	Green
Wading	Green	Parking	Green
Shore Fishing	Yellow	Regulations	Yellow
Spin Fishing	Green	Fly Fishing	Green
Scenery	Yellow	Overall	Yellow

Special Regulations

None.

Getting to the Stream

From Virginia: Northbound on Rt 17 from Virginia, cross the river and continue to the traffic circle in Brunswick. Take the second exit from the circle onto East A Street.

From Maryland: From US 340 going west from Frederick, turn south on Rt 17 at the Burkittsville exit. At the traffic circle that marks the junction with Rt 180, take the second exit to stay on Rt 17 and follow that into town. At the traffic circle in town, take the fourth exit onto East A Street.

Turn right on North Maple Ave and follow it across the train tracks. When it dead ends on a dirt road, turn right and follow it to the boat launch.

There is plenty of parking. The lot overlooks a small side channel of the river. If you want to start fishing right here, splash across the shallow water to cross the narrow island and reach the main river.

Environment and Fish

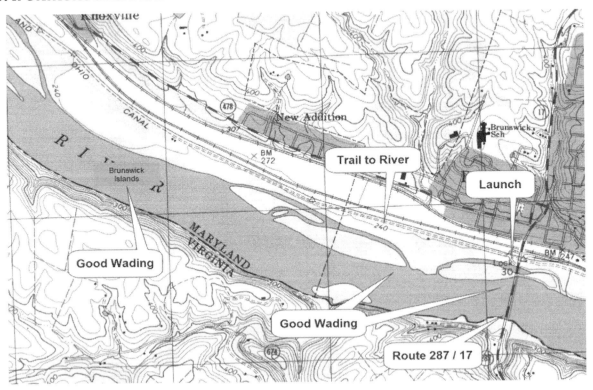

The Brunswick boat launch is a good place to wade. I personally prefer going upstream to the Brunswick Islands that you can see in the Google satellite view at 39.315773,-77.656839.

The first option is to slosh across the shallow backwater that separates the concrete launch pad from the main river channel; cross the small island and wade into the water. You can begin fishing your way upstream from that point.

Once you start to fish, you'll be pleased to see that the bottom structure is perfect for smallmouth bass. The bottom is uniformly rocky with randomly dispersed deeper areas protected by rock ledges that run perpendicular to the shoreline. You can fish your way out into the center of the channel without any problem at all when the river is running at levels acceptable for wading (1.60 ft at Point of Rocks). The area immediately around the boat launch will experience the greatest amount of pressure. One approach to get away from the high traffic area is to take advantage of the easy walking on the towpath to move away from the launch and then cut back over to the river to fish in a more remote location.

If you follow this strategy, you have two options. One involves following the towpath to 39.313416,-77.64081; approximately a half mile up from the launch site. At that point, there is a beaten, narrow trail that provides easy access to the river. Follow the path to the intersection with the backwater separating the large island you see on the map from the main shoreline. The path runs left along the top of the steep bank and winds its way around the tip of the island (39.31105,-77.638772). There is a shallow shelf that extends a significant distance out into the river and you can move either upstream to the Brunswick Islands from here or fish downstream to the boat launch. In either direction, the shoreline structure is ideal and consists of overhanging branches and fallen trees that provide shelter for fish. Some pretty good sized smallmouth like to hang in the shade thrown off by the tall trees along the shoreline during the heat of the day. Otherwise, keep your attention on the deeper cuts and runs that you will have to discover in the main channel by either stumbling across them or looking for the slightly darker color that indicates deeper water.

Late in the summer, the area immediately around the boat launch is clogged with vegetation that grows to the surface of the water and waves lazily downstream for several feet. To fish this, target the open spots that border a deeper hole or a rock ledge. In general, if the water is moving faster, like it will up by the Brunswick Islands, there is not as much vegetation. If you prefer fishing in less congested water, put on your walking shoes and walk the extra distance upstream.

Assuming you don't mind the hike on the towpath to get to the Brunswick Islands, your next challenge will be to determine where to cut over to the river. There is no well-defined path from the towpath to the good fishing. Instead, walk 1.4 miles from the launch area to 39.318213,-77.655616. Set your bearings and bushwhack south to the river. The brush is pretty thick here, so leave your rod disassembled until you actually reach the river. You may also want to carry a small pair of garden snips to help you get through some of the vines whose only purpose is to slow you down.

This is the view up river from 39.31105,-77.638772.

The shoreline is tight going upstream and limits the opportunity to fish from the shore. If you're going to fish upstream from here, you have to wade.

The Point of Rocks gage was running at 1.23 ft when this picture was taken.

This is the view downstream back to the bridge.

You can fish from the shore if you want to, but the shore parallels a shallow shelf that runs out to the center of the river.

There are a limited number of deeper cuts that will hold fish within casting range of the shore.

Be prepared to bushwhack through undergrowth that looks like this since there are few trails from the towpath to the river.

In thick brush, it is easy to become disoriented and wander off course.

Be sure you take a compass or a GPS with you to stay on track.

Bottom line

I like the entire Brunswick area. The river has a calm character to it that makes fishing here a serene and passive experience.

Knoxville Falls

Google Map Coordinates: 39.329451,-77.682567

Summary Rating

Pressure	Red	Canoe/Kayak Launch	Red
Physical Fitness	Red	Trailer Boat Launch	Red
Wading	Green	Parking	Red
Shore Fishing	Green	Regulations	Yellow
Spin Fishing	Green	Fly Fishing	Green
Scenery	Green	Overall	Green

Special Regulations

None.

Getting to the Stream

From Virginia: From US 340, turn east on MD 180 at the stoplight just north of the bridge over the Potomac. MD 180 becomes Keep Tryst Road.

From Maryland: From US 340, get off at the Boonsboro exit (MD-67) and make a U-turn to get back onto US 340 heading east. Immediately after the joining the highway, turn right onto Keep Tryst Road (there will not be an off ramp; it's just a right turn).

Regardless of how you get onto Keep Tryst Road, follow it until you come to a sharp bend adjacent to the railroad tracks. At the bend, you might be tempted to drive through the gate, and cross the tracks to park adjacent to the towpath. DO NOT do that! There is a very small sign on the gate that says "No motor vehicles" and you could be locked in. That almost happened to me. I drove through the open gate, never saw the sign and happened to ask another guy if it was ok to park here. He recommended I park back on the road. I am glad I followed his advice because the gate was locked when I came back out! Parking is limited to the shoulders of the road and will fit approximately ten vehicles comfortably.

To reach the river, follow the access road through the gate and across the railroad tracks. You can see the towpath from the parking area. Walk over and make your first decision. If you follow the beaten path that runs perpendicular away from the towpath behind the C&O Canal NHP signs, it will take you to the river just above Knoxville Falls. Alternatively, turn right and walk north for a mile to fish the area leading up to the US 340 bridge.

Environment and Fish

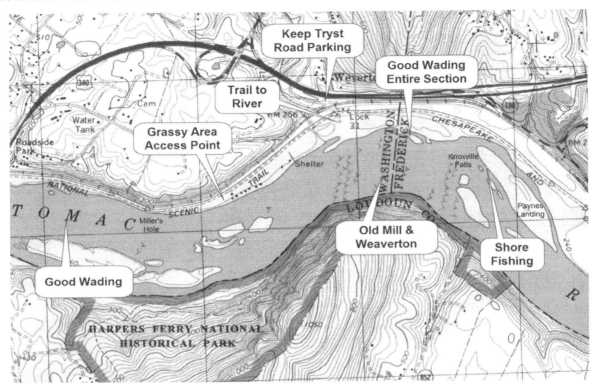

Upstream

Assuming you made the decision to turn right and head upstream, stay on the towpath until you arrive at a broad, grassy area on the left at 39.323276,-77.690109. Walk down to the shoreline and wade into the river to fish upstream. If you continue west on the towpath, there are several faint trails that lead to the river at various alternative entry points. However, the bank west of the grassy area is abrupt and steep with precipitous hillsides leading to the narrow shoreline. Therefore, the grassy area is the best place to start.

At the grassy area, the river is not overly deep and it puts you onto a nice rocky ledge that runs perpendicular to the shoreline. Like every other place in this section of the Potomac, you cannot wade directly up and downstream. The rock ledges form boundaries between deep water on either side. Your fishing experience will consist of finding a ledge, walking out on it, fishing and then returning to the shoreline to repeat this at the next ledge.

Given the depth, wear a PFD; especially if you are wearing waders. You could easily slip off one of the ridges and find yourself instantly in over your head -- the water is that deep! The depth also demands a tailored approach to fishing. If you are spin fishing, use weighted lures to get down and bump on the bottom. If you are fly fishing, be sure and bring a sinking tip to get your streamer to the bottom. You could use a full sinking line, but it limits your flexibility for other presentations. You can use dry flies and poppers in the area closer to the shore, but most of your fishing moving upstream will be in deep water. If you want to go on top, use size 4 poppers and fish them next to the ridge as you move out.

Upstream from the grassy area, the shoreline consists of a narrow band of sand -- a foot or two wide -- that slams into a vertical bank. You may find yourself clinging to the dense thickets and trees growing out of the bank to keep your balance as you move upstream. At lower water levels, the edge of the shoreline is easily wadeable. At higher flows, you may actually have to go all the way back to the towpath to move upstream since there is a channel that cuts a deep gouge next to the shoreline limiting your flexibility.

A short distance upstream (39.323625,-77.696686), the river slows as it pushes through a slight bend on the Maryland side called Miller's Hole. It shallows out and you can wade quickly across to the main channel without having to be on a ledge. Fifty yards upstream from Miller's Hole there is a small island that is separated slightly from the shore. Once you are even with it, walk towards the center of the river until you encounter a long rock ledge running parallel to the river at 39.323554,-77.699293.

Fish that spot hard. It's deep and fast. Fly anglers should use heavily weighted, large nymphs such as a Bitch Creek (size 8 – 12) and target the deep slot on the Virginia side of the ledge.

Spin fisherman will not have a problem as it will be easy to work a weighted plastic grub or Senko to the bottom. According to locals, black is the preferred color within a mile of the bridge. Since the water is frequently muddy in this area as a result of the silt piling into the Potomac from the Shenandoah junction just upstream, it's easy to see how this would be the right choice. However, if the water is clear, change your attack to use natural colored plastics.

Don't bother to fish the Maryland shoreline from the bridge down to this point. It's generally shallow and unproductive. Stick to the middle as much as you can. Once you finish working the parallel ledge, there is one last perpendicular ledge closer to the bridge that requires your attention. It is located near another large island on the Maryland shore. Wade up to it and move back out into the river on the ledge at approximately 39.324173,-77.701825.

As you teter on the ledge and look towards Harpers Ferry, you will see other anglers working the rock ridges that surround the bridge itself. There are better access points to use to fish the areas near the bridge than walking up from the Keep Tryst Road parking area.

This is the view upstream on a great summer day from just around the bend at Miller's Hole west of the grassy park in the vicinity of 39.323144,-77.69263.

The water level at the Point of Rocks gage was only 1.07 ft when this picture was taken and represents a best case perspective on the amount of visible structure.

The tall trees at the far right are on the island that marks the start point of the last good ledge stretching to Virginia from the Maryland side below the US 340 bridge.

This picture was taken looking over deep water; you still need to work your way up the shoreline for another 50 yards before arriving at a shallow, sandy area that facilitates movement back to the center of the river.

This is the area around the bend from the grassy area where the river shallows out and slows down as it gathers energy to career round the corner.

The angler pictured here could move another 25 yards to the right and still be in slow water.

The rock ledge in the distance in this picture is the last, good ledge stretching out from the Maryland side near the grassy area.

The next good perpendicular ledge is near the US 340 bridge.

Straight Out

Once you reach the shore by following the heavily traveled dirt trail from the towpath, you find yourself looking at one of the best sections on the entire Potomac. From the shoreline, there are many visible clusters of perpendicular ridges that provide quick access to the center of the river; some of them even run all the way to Virginia. Assuming the picture was not taken when the river was in flood, a quick look at the Google satellite picture at 39.327127,-77.680206 tells you everything you need to know! When you look at the satellite view showing the spider's web of ridges that spread out like cracks in broken glass, you can't help but feel your adrenaline start to rush, your blood pump and your pupils narrow; there have to be big fish here. There are. Unfortunately, the best access to those fish comes to those who are willing to wade. The shoreline, while good, does not put you on exceptional water. The main current of the river and the concentration of smallmouth are farther out from the Maryland shore than you can cast.

Fishing this section is a matter of picking a ridge and walking out; being careful of the fast water moving between the taller rocks. Like the upstream section, the water is uniformly deep on both sides of the ridges. However, it is not as deep as it is farther upstream. Fly anglers do not need to resort to a sinking tip. Just crimp a split shot or two above your streamer. There are plenty of shallow areas where you can deploy a size 6 popper and have good action all day.

Spin fisherman will have a good time with the typical bottom bumping plastics as well as small crank baits. There are wide pools between the rock ridges that allow you to deploy a crankbait that goes 3 to 5 feet down and not run the risk of hanging up on the bottom.

Twenty five yards down from where the trail hits the river, the main ridge that is the primary terrain feature in this area joins the shore. It's called the Weaverton Ledge and was built in the last century by Casper Weaver in a failed attempt to channel water to power his planned industrial complex. You can still see twisted metal mixed in with the large rocks and concrete that form the ridge. His failure is our joy as the ledge creates the perfect perch from which to launch attacks on some of the best smallmouth in the river. If somebody is already fishing Weaverton, walk another twenty five yards downriver to the next major ledge. It's called the Old Mill Ledge and the water that sits upstream between it and Weaverton is probably the best place to fish in the whole river. On a good day, with the water at the right level and the right clarity, you could spend your entire afternoon walking back and forth on these ridges. Granted their existence is not a secret and plenty of people fish from these; making this the most heavily pressured section of the river. However, it seems like most people abide by a catch and release ethic that maintains the quality of the fishery. I encourage you to do the same.

The area immediately downstream of Old Mill Ledge is hazardous since it is directly upstream of Knoxville Falls. Knoxville Falls is not a falls in the sense of Niagara Falls, but it is a significant feature on the river that demands caution. I have fished from Old Mill and watched people wade almost all the way to the Virginia side, dancing across rocks and boulders, downstream of the ledge to get to the deeper pools below. I recommend you do not take that risk since that section has a large number of deep holes joined by a fast current. You could find yourself swept off your feet and launched on an exciting ride over the short stretch of falls just downstream.

If the two main ledges are busy, walk upstream from the trailhead and fish out on any of the large number of smaller, unnamed ridges that run perpendicular to the shoreline. The fishing they offer is equally as good as the formally named ledges although you will spend more time in the water since they do not have the same volume of rocks to lift them above the surface. Plan your moves carefully as you creep along these ledges. You should wear a PFD.

This is the view upstream from just above the junction of the trail with the river at 39.327351,-77.681762.

Upstream of the main ledges, there are less prominent perpendicular extrusions.

It becomes a little sportier to stay on top of them when the water is covering most of their bulk.

Be sure you use a wading staff and wear a PFD in this area. This picture was taken when the Point of Rocks gage was running at a low 1.23 ft.

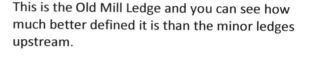

This is the Old Mill Ledge and you can see how much better defined it is than the minor ledges upstream.

Moving out on Old Mill or Weaverton gives you a broad path and countless good options that do not involve wading in deep water.

This is the broad pool that separates Old Mill from Weaverton.

Weaverton is the line of rocks in the center of the picture and is an obvious and easy way to move a significant distance into the center of the river.

The Point of Rocks gage reading was 0.99 ft when this picture was taken and demonstrates the optimum conditions.

The area downstream of Old Mill that leads into the Knoxville Falls is too risky for me to want to wade.

Granted, you can see plenty of structure and ridges, but the current starts to move fast as it darts left to go down the falls.

Knoxville Falls

After discussing the great fishing at the trailhead as well as upstream to the US 340 bridge, it's a little bit depressing to comment on the actual Knoxville Falls area. This is a small area bounded by Old Mill Ledge and the bend downstream between Paynes Landing and Falls Island that leads into the Brunswick Islands that are midway between Knoxville Falls and the Brunswick boat launch.

As I mentioned above, I do not recommend wading below the Old Mill Ledge. Although there are ridges that facilitate your movement, the current gets fast and there are deep pockets. The danger, given the proximity of Knoxville Falls, is not worth it.

When you reach the river at the trailhead, turn left to amble on the small winding path that leads to the base of Knoxville Falls. As a warm-up, fish the shallow shelf that stretches out from the shore for about 25 to 30 yards before you get into the faster moving water. There are several pockets that run 2 to 3 feet deep that hold considerable numbers of small smallmouth. Of course, you can catch sunfish all day long.

At the base of the falls, you have a choice of fishing down the side channel that splits Paynes Landing from the shore or wading across to Paynes Landing and fish downstream in the main river. The side channel shallows out, becoming sandy in places, and does not embody a top-notch fishing opportunity when compared to the other areas in the immediate vicinity. The main channel, on the other hand, presents insurmountable challenges to wading. Waders are restricted to the few rock ledges that poke weakly into the main current. On the other hand, this is a great spot to fish from the shore if you are willing to wade across the side channel to reach Paynes Landing.

Fly anglers should use a sinking tip or full sinking line to get streamers to the bottom. Spin fisherman will have no problem using any of the lures at their disposal given the depth of the water. The best approach for either type of angler is to get the lure down as quickly as possible, maintain a tight line, twitching and letting it drift downstream with the current.

This is the view downstream towards Knoxville Falls from the terminus of the trail leading to the river.

Use the path on the shore or fish the shallow water near the bank on the way to the falls.

The ridgeline in the distance marks Knoxville Falls. The main flow of the water is to the left towards Maryland.

This is Knoxville Falls looking upstream on a day when the Point of Rocks gage read 1.23 ft.

In higher flow conditions, the Falls can be hazardous; driving the requirement to wear a PFD.

This is the side channel that splits Paynes Landing from the Maryland shore.

It gets pretty shallow and is not worth fishing.

On the typical weekend day, bass boats will come all the way up to the base of the falls.

For obvious reasons, powerboats can't go above Knoxville Falls unless they are under the control of an expert or a crazy person.

Note the few rocky protrusions sticking out from the Maryland shore on the left.

Bottom Line

If I had to pick my favorite place on the entire river, it would be Knoxville Falls. The great variety of structure combined with the mix of shallow and deep water establish the perfect environment for some of the best bass fishing you will ever experience. The only negative associated with this area is that large carp enjoy teasing you as they leap out of the water, creating a huge slapping splash, and you immediately assume that you are missing out on massive smallies just out of your reach. But, the big bass are here and they can be found in the shallower water near the ledges ... when they do that -- hold on!

Harpers Ferry

Google Map Coordinates: 39.325368,-77.738872

Summary Rating

Pressure	**Red**	Canoe/Kayak Launch	**Yellow**
Physical Fitness	**Red**	Trailer Boat Launch	**Red**
Wading	**Green**	Parking	**Red**
Shore Fishing	**Green**	Regulations	**Yellow**
Spin Fishing	**Green**	Fly Fishing	**Green**
Scenery	**Green**	Overall	**Green**

Special Regulations

Be alert for the border of West Virginia and Virginia since it triggers a change in regulations. If you have a Maryland fishing license, you can fish the entire Harpers Ferry area without concern as a result of reciprocal agreements Maryland has with both Virginia and West Virginia. If you only have a West Virginia or Virginia license, be sure you stay within the boundary of that state or be aware of where you are in relation to your State if fishing from the Maryland side.

There is a set of power lines crossing the river near the US 340 bridge that are approximately 1,000 feet upstream of the border between Virginia and West Virginia. You can use those as a rough landmark to make sure you are fishing legally based on the State that issued your license.

Remember that Maryland regulations govern behavior on the river. All three States have agreed to abide by the limits established by Maryland.

The Shenandoah is not part of the reciprocal agreement with Maryland. If you want to fish the Shenandoah, you need a West Virginia license.

Harpers Ferry is a very popular area and is well patrolled by conservation officers who are experts on where your license is good; so you need to be equally well informed!

General Comment

Harpers Ferry is a smallmouth bass angler's dream location. There are many different access points, each of which offers a slightly different fishing experience as well as requiring a different set of directions to put you on the water. I'll cover each of these in detail by first working up the Maryland side and then flipping over to Virginia; ending in the town of Harpers Ferry.

Harpers Ferry East End Map

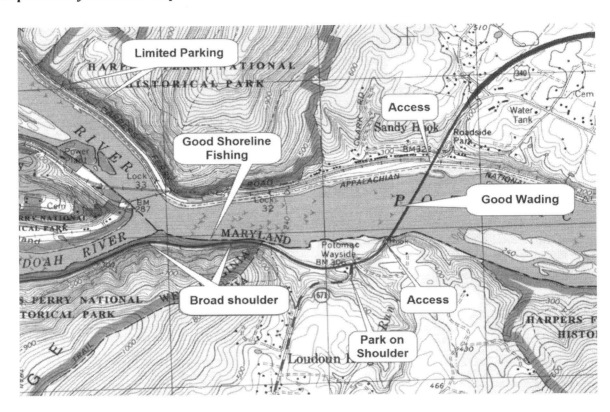

Harpers Ferry West End Map

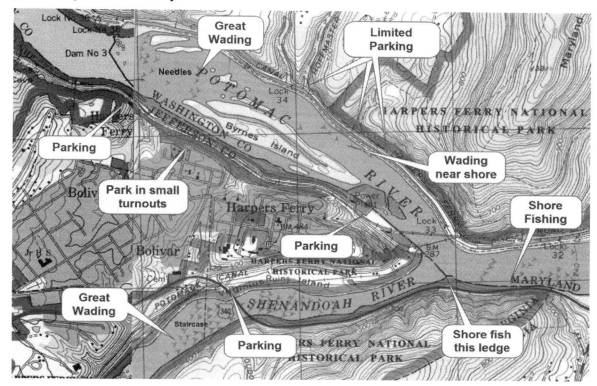

Maryland 340 Bridge

Google Map Coordinates: 39.325534,-77.707844

Getting to the Stream

From US 340, turn east on MD 180 at the stoplight just north of the bridge. Follow it for a short distance (it will join Keep Tryst Road) and turn right on Sandy Hook Road to roll down a steep hill that leads under the bridge. Turn around and park on the shoulder next to the railroad tracks. Do not block the service road on the north side of the street that leads up to a maintenance facility that is hidden behind a wall of cypress trees.

The trail to the river is not obvious since it is hidden by the railroad tracks. Use the big rock pictured below as a landmark. Once you find it, cross the tracks to intersect the broad, beaten trail that leads directly to one of the spans of the 340 bridge.

The view east to the bridge shows the small grocery store on the left. You can park here or in the smaller shoulder area closer to the bridge.

This is a nice little store where you can pick up a sandwich and something to drink. They need your business and I encourage you to stop in and support them.

This is the rock that is the landmark marking the right place to cross the tracks to find the trail to the river.

Go across the railroad tracks (being careful since this is an active railway) and continue down the broad trail leading to the river.

The trail is hard to miss and provides a straight shot to the river; ending directly under the bridge span.

If you park in a different location or cannot find the large rock, walk up the tracks towards the bridge span – it would be difficult to miss this trail.

If you do not want to enter the river at the bridge, your next opportunity is west of Sandy Hook.

In Sandy Hook, the underbrush on the river side of the tracks (shown here) is dense and thick. Even though there is plenty of parking on the shoulder, you'll have a tough time bushwhacking your way through.

The best tactic if you want to fish alongside of Sandy Hook is to park near the bridge and use the towpath to move farther upstream.

This spot picks up where we left the story upstream from Knoxville Falls and is a key takeout location for kayakers. Therefore, you should expect a significant amount of company during warm days in summer and move away from the access point to get to undisturbed water.

There is good wading up and downriver from the bridge. During periods of low water, you can actually walk all the way over to Virginia. Your first inclination should be to move down river and work your way along the defined ridge you'll see poking up 50 yards below the bridge.

The experience upstream is essentially the same although you need to move away from the shore into center of the river. There is a shallow shelf stretching from the base of the bridge that you need to cross before the fishing improves.

This is mostly a wade fishing location. The trees are thick along the shoreline and, while you can twist your way between them, it will be in more trouble than it is worth. Of course, the towpath parallels the river and you can use it to skip from place to place as you look for open areas that permit you to fish from the shore. The better fishing is available by wading since you can get farther out and fish the channels that are formed by the rock ridges and the boulders that litter this area.

In terms of gear, either type of fishing attack is effective. Both spin and fly approaches will work just fine. Fly anglers have the additional advantage of being able to fish some of the structure closer to the shore with small poppers that always produce explosive strikes. Just like downstream, you need to be able to get your lure down below the surface for the best results. If the water is moving fast, an intermediate sink tip is a good idea if you are fly angler; you do not need a full sinking tip line.

This is the view looking up river from the base of the bridge.

The scattered grass provides a sense of the shallow shelf that stretches towards West Virginia.

The shelf extends beyond the base of the pylon on the left.

Downstream shows better water and more structure.

Interestingly enough, the island on the left is posted and is marked as such by the blue blazes on the tree trunks. Therefore, pick someplace else if you want to have a picnic or take a break.

You can also see the beginnings of the downstream ridge -- use that to orient your fishing.

This is another view of the downstream stretch from the bridge. Below the ridge, the river flattens out and is uniformly three feet or better in depth.

You have to pick your path carefully to move downstream.

Sandy Hook Road

Google Map Coordinates: 39.32928,-77.73185, 39.33033,-77.73385, 39.33331,-77.73850

Getting to the Stream

From Rt 7 coming out of Northern Virginia, turn onto the Charlestown Pike. Take 671 (Harpers Ferry Road) and follow it north until it crosses the river at Harpers Ferry. Take the first right (Keep Tryst Road) followed by another right on Sandy Hook road. Continue on the road past the sharp turn at the railroad bridge.

You might be tempted to park at the single vehicle pullout on the right at the base of the railroad bridge but don't. The only bridges across the canal between the corner and where the road turns north to run to Pleasantville are near several small parking areas scattered along the route.

Once you round the bend at the railroad bridge, there are two turnouts along the road; each of which holds approximately ten vehicles (39.32928,-77.73185, 39.33033,-77.73385), and a final turnout where the road bends north that has room for three (39.33331,-77.73850). You have to be here early in the day to get a spot if you come on a weekend since this is a popular place for hordes of hikers and bikers in addition to anglers.

Parking is tight in the small turnouts.

If you can't find a parking place in one of the turnouts, you are in for some exercise.

You can still get access to this area by parking in Sandy Hook and walking or biking up the towpath.

This is the small turnout at the end of the road (39.33331,-77.73850).

The road bends away from the river to the right.

This spot is primarily a loading and unloading zone with limited parking. Do not park illegally since it is heavily patrolled.

This is a great place to fish up towards Dam 3.

Environment and Fish

The fishing experience changes depending on where you park. A quick word of caution is that you will not have a solitary fishing day anywhere in Harpers Ferry. Not only is it popular with other anglers, but there will be plenty of tubers, kayakers and canoeists floating through your fishing hole. Given the proximity of the towpath, this is the perfect place to bring a bike to find less pressured areas. I recommend that you not try to wade near the ruins of the old railroad bridge in the vicinity of 39.323625,-77.727048 since the river compresses as it charges around the corner to slam into the Shenandoah. This area stays deep even at periods of low flow. In addition to poor access for wading, the bank is steep and full of trees that prevent shoreline fishers from moving freely. Therefore, move upstream into the "needles" area or downstream back to the US 340 bridge.

In general, the river below where the road bends north towards Pleasantville is consistently flat. Anglers walk out on broad, slick ledges to perch next to the main flow of the river and fish the channels. Each of the rock ledges is separated by a small lake filled with still water that only holds sunfish. The smallmouth bass will be where the water is moving. Depending on where you enter, you can get a decent distance out into the river on the ledges.

The area upriver from where the road turns north is the tailwater associated with Dam 3 called the "needles." As it spills over the dam, the river forms two swift channels; one running down the Maryland shore with a mirror image scrubbing West Virginia. The water moves fast over a slick bottom, so use a wading staff to keep from falling and joining the tubers floating downstream. Once across, work your way up the outer perimeter of the middle area, fishing the deeper water of the channel. Do this all the way up to the Dam 3. After you move away from the channel, you find yourself on a broad island that is sliced by many fast-moving channels feeding into shallow holes. You can pick up small smallmouth bass and as many sunfish as you care to catch in the middle area.

There is one deep spot at the bottom end of the needles that holds good, large fish. You can have a lot of fun fishing this section with fly gear since the sunfish and smallmouth are always anxious to chew on dry flies and poppers. Spin fisherman may become frustrated in the needles using anything other than weedless presentations as a result of the shallow water conspiring with the rocky bottom to snag unprotected hooks.

Shoreline fishing in this area is problematic given the shallow shelf that stretches from the Maryland shore. You have to move away from the steep bank to find any fishable water. If you are not willing to wade, you should not come here.

If you park at either of the two turnouts, the nearby river is expansive and flat.

At the far right, the river gathers back together for the straight shot down to the junction with the Shenandoah after being fractured by the innumerable rock ridges of the needles below Dam 3.

Looking downstream, many rock ledges stretch their fingers out into the heart of the river.

These offer good, quick access with a minimal amount of wading.

This is the tight, fast channel that barrels down the Maryland shoreline from Dam 3. The rocky outcroppings of the needles are at the left of the picture.

Depending on the volume of water, it can be tricky to cross and you need to be careful. Pick your spot well.

The Point of Rocks gage was running at 1.23 ft when this picture was taken and it was a minor

struggle to cross.

This is the needles– it's a wonderland of great, shallow channels leading to pools (usually 2 -3 feet deep) that hold sunfish and small bass.

You can spend a good afternoon working this area. Be sure to go all the way up to Dam 3.

Virginia – 340 Bridge

Google Map Coordinates: 39.320023,-77.712007

Getting to the Stream

North: From Frederick, MD, the directions are pretty simple. Get on US 340 heading south and stay on it until you cross the Potomac River.

South: From Leesburg, VA, head west on VA 7. Take the VA 9 offramp to Hillsboro/Charlestown and merge onto VA 9 W. Turn right on Harpers Ferry Rd (SR 671) and follow it to the intersection with US 340.

From either direction, the access point for fishing is 25 yards west of the bridge on the Virginia side. As you drive by, you will see a small turnout peppered with "no parking" signs marking the access point. The Park Service permits loading and unloading, but you are not allowed to park for any length of time. Parking is a problem; particularly if you get to the river late.

There are two places you should not park. The first is to take a space in the gas station at the corner. They have a prolific number of signs limiting parking to 15 minutes and, when asked, they told me that they enforce that policy.

The second place to avoid is the wide turnout on the left immediately west of the gas station on the road to Harpers Ferry (39.319475,-77.715054). It is posted as private property and signs caution the unwary against parking there.

I chatted with a popcorn vendor who told me that he and other vendors rent space in the turnout from the property owner. Cars parked on the east side of the lot (where his popcorn stand is) may be towed by the owner or blocked in by vendors. I was told that the owner allows a few cars to park at the far west end. My conclusion is that is not a safe bet and unless you are a risk taker, you should stick to the shoulders.

The Catoctin Popcorn Company has GREAT popcorn. Stop and get a bag of the kettle variety – it is my favorite of the many varieties they offer.

The good news is that there are wide shoulders and plenty of spaces on SR 671. It comes up from the south to intersect US 340 and the 50 yards leading up to the stop light offer plenty of room on the shoulders. At the date of publication, there were not any "no parking" signs along the road. According to the people in the gas station, folks routinely park on the shoulders of both SR 671 and US 340.

Once you find a parking spot, walk back to the loading/unloading zone to the gap in the rock wall that is the opening for the sheer trail to the river.

This is the small turnout for loading and unloading (39.320023,-77.712007). Note the numerous no parking signs as well as the warnings about towing.

The path to the river is immediately to the right. The stoplight at the upper left is the intersection of SR 671 and US 340.

There is plenty of parking on the shoulders of SR 671.

The trail to the river is broad, smooth and scenic with a small waterfall to the left at the bottom of the hill (not worth fishing).

This is a key launch/takeout point for canoes and kayaks and the Park Service has done a good job of maintaining the trail to facilitate portage up the steep hill to the loading zone.

The wading near the US 340 bridge is much better than what unfolds on the Maryland shore. The shoreline fishing is marginal given the shallow water from here down to and below the bridge. Beyond the immediate vicinity of the launch, the shoreline is heavily vegetated and people who do not want to get their feet wet will end up bushwhacking to reach places where they can fish in water that is deep enough to be productive. For shore fishers, you should move up river on US 340 to the broad turnout that is just beyond the border with West Virginia. In that location, the water is deep and the shoreline accessible.

Once you reach the bridge, there is no trail leading to the east. The property beyond the bridge is privately owned until you get to the vicinity of 39.32000, -77.70274 (approximately 900 feet downstream of the bridge). Even if it were not, the bank is steep, cliff-like, and limits further movement downstream on the shore. Depending upon the water levels, you can continue to move downriver if you are willing to wade.

Moving north from the launch, public property continues until you reach 39.32082,-77.717628 at which point it becomes private for a short distance; flipping back to public just beyond the border with West Virginia.
Your best approach for fishing is to wade directly out from either the launch or walk down to the bridge and move into the water from there. There are plenty of shallow areas bordered by broad rock shelves that allow you to scramble out as far into the river as you care to go. Depending on the conditions, you may have to move up or downstream to work around the deep channels. To move across the river, stick to the major ridges.

Neither fly nor spin fishers will have any problems in this area. Fishing with either method requires movement away from the shoreline to find deeper water that holds bass. Fly fishers will have the advantage in shallow areas where they can flip poppers up against the shoreline as well as in the thin pools that collect behind some of the protruding boulders.

This is the view looking up the river from the canoe takeout. The broad pool is actually a shallow shelf that extends a good distance into the river.

You can wade out from here if you want.

The line of rocks at the top of the picture is the rapid called the "washing machine."

This is the view downriver from the same position.

The great rock structure channels the water and makes movement into the center of the river easier.

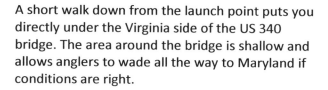

A short walk down from the launch point puts you directly under the Virginia side of the US 340 bridge. The area around the bridge is shallow and allows anglers to wade all the way to Maryland if conditions are right.

If you have time, you should cross the bridge using the pedestrian walkway and do a visual recon of the water. In short order, you will identify the good spots to target and the best path to get there; they are visible from above.

US 340 West Virginia / Virginia Border

Google Map Coordinates: 39.32117,-77.71965

Getting to the Stream

North: From Frederick, MD, the directions are pretty simple. Get on US 340 heading south and stay on it until you cross the Potomac River. Continue on US 340 towards Harpers Ferry.

South: From Leesburg, VA, head west on VA 7. Take the VA 9 offramp to Hillsboro/Charlestown and merge onto VA 9 W. Turn right on Harpers Ferry Rd (SR 671) and follow it to the intersection with US 340. Turn left and head towards Harper's Ferry.

Once you cross into West Virginia, the road adds a wide, long shoulder next to the river that appears to be explicitly designed to handle the traffic associated with river activities (39.32117,-77.71965). Although the bank is steep, there are numerous beaten paths that lead to the river; all of them require a climb over rocks that are slick when wet.

This stretch of the Potomac is perfect for shoreline fishing. Although the drop-off from the road and is steep and requires a careful climb over the rocks, once you reach the shoreline, it's wide enough to allow lateral movement. Most of the water runs fast and deep except for the few places where several large and dramatic ledges leap from the shore towards Maryland.

If you decide to wade, your access is limited to broad rock ridges. They stretch most of the way across the river and you must be careful working your way through the gaps in the ridges where the river frantically pushes the added velocity and volume of the water contributed by the Shenandoah just upstream. What is an obstacle for an angler is a playground for a kayaker! These locations earned their names - "Surprise Rapids", "Mad Dog Rapids", "Whitehorse Rapids" and the "Washing Machine" - prime whitewater for kayakers. This is an area of class III or IV rapids given the correct water conditions. Your best shot at getting out into the river is to walk to the Virginia end of the broad turnout. That's where the "Washing Machine" stretches towards Maryland. This is a complex, convoluted and broad rock formation. It's full of twists and turns with deep channels. The pools both up and downstream are highly productive; cast as far into them as you can. Don't do anything stupid as you move on this ledge -- accept the fact that you will be closed out and not able to get as far into the river (or at all) as you would like. You can confirm the quality of this area for yourself by popping open the satellite view of this section of the river in Google Maps - 39.322231,-77.717843.

One place you may want to spend some time is at the junction of the Shenandoah with the Potomac. Continue up US 340 to another large turnout (39.32074,-77.72892) where the road bends west in its approach to the Shenandoah bridge. Move to the western end of the parking lot where there is a "sporty-looking" wide spot between the bushes that gives you access to a rocky, steep, dim trail leading down the embankment to the broad ledge that marks the junction of the two rivers. The ledge is visible and fishable even when the water is above what is nominally considered "normal." When you move out onto the broad ledge, you can fish the deep water where the Shenandoah joins the Potomac and then flip over and fish the Potomac side.

The best type of tackle to use if you're confined to the shoreline is spin gear. If you are a fly angler, you have to get out into the river to have adequate room for your backcast. The steep bank is only a few feet behind you and limits your ability to push the fly a significant distance into the river. The water is deep and you need to use an intermediate sink tip or even a full sinking line depending on the specific water conditions you encounter. There are a few randomly dispersed shallow areas mixed in with the ridge structure, but most of your fishing in this section will be deep. Spin fishers can use the entire range of gear from crankbaits and spinners to plastic lures.

This is a typical path leading down to the shoreline.

Note the steep pitch as well as the fact that it flattens out into boulder strewn bank that is approximately 20 feet wide.

Although the 20 foot border between the road and river is not guaranteed throughout the entire stretch, there is enough maneuver room to allow you to move in either direction.

View downstream from the shoreline between the rapids. The water runs deep; not wadeable.

The Point of Rocks gage was running at 1.68 ft when this picture was taken.

The water was high when this picture was taken but you can still see the well-defined ridge structure of the "Washing Machine."

The Point of Rocks gage was running above normal at 2.7 feet.

The view of Mad Dog Rapids at above normal flow.

Don't try and move onto any of the ledges in this area if the river is running high and fast. The rocks are slippery and you can find yourself swept downstream.

Wear a PFD if you fish this section.

This is a broad ledge that marks the boundary between the Shenandoah on the left and the Potomac on the right. Once you climb down, it's easy walk out on this ledge and fish both sides of river.

Remember that you need a West Virginia license to fish on the Shenandoah side of this ledge. Your Maryland license is good on the Potomac side.

Shenandoah – 340 Bridge

Google Map Coordinates: 39.32164,-77.74300

Getting to the Stream

North: From Frederick, MD, the directions are pretty simple. Get on US 340 heading south and stay on it until you cross the Potomac River. Continue on US 340 towards Harpers Ferry.

South: From Leesburg, VA, head west on VA 7. Take the VA 9 off ramp to Hillsboro/Charlestown and merge onto VA 9 W. Turn right on Harpers Ferry Rd (SR 671) and follow it to the intersection with US 340. Turn left and head towards Harper's Ferry.

US 340 parallels the river, winding around precipitous mountains to eventually cross the Shenandoah River on the outskirts of Harpers Ferry. Take a hard right immediately after crossing the river and drive down the short hill to the parking lot that marks one of the entrances to the Harpers Ferry National Historical Park. There is a fee to park in the lot … with a wrinkle. There is no attendant in the lot. Instead, you place the parking fee in an envelope available from the kiosk and display the receipt in your windshield. The sign that provides guidance on what to pay specifically says that anglers and boaters are exempt from paying the parking fee. I have no idea how an enforcement officer would go from car to car and decide which vehicle belongs to an angler versus a normal tourist. Therefore, I recommend you pay the fee anyway as it goes to a good cause -- maintaining the Park. If you decide not to pay the fee, you should put a sign in your windshield indicating that you are fishing. When you arrive, double check at the kiosk to make sure the rules have not changed.

To get to the river, walk up the short hill and through the gate towards the base of the bridge. The Superintendent's Compendium (the document that further refines the regulatory wording flowing down to the Park from federal regulations) establishes the clear fact that:

> "There is established a river access corridor to provide access to the Shenandoah River for river recreation purposes. The corridor extends from the parking area at the end of Shenandoah Street (intersection with Rt. 340) to the upstream side of the Rt. 340 bridge. For the purpose of this regulation the River access corridor shall be defined as an area extending 50 yards on either side of the trail leading from the parking lot to the river shore."

I checked with the Chief Ranger of the Harpers Ferry NHP and he confirmed that this language is still in effect. This means that the CSX railroad cannot prohibit access.

Go through the gate and across the tracks to the shoreline.

It's an easy, gentle walk.

If other members of your party want to visit the tourist attractions, they should stick to the path that is on the river side of the main road. There is no path towards Harpers Ferry beyond the gate.

Once you reach the river, your adrenaline will pump as you look across the wide expanse of rock ledges that extend to the horizon. This section is called the "staircase" with the best fishing stretching upstream from the bridge. While you can move downstream, you run into the "Cotton Mill Rapids", a Class II rapid, that is followed by the "Rollercoaster" Class III rapids. This is a popular playground for kayakers. In to maintain the historic character of the Park, the section of the river from the bridge downstream to the junction was declared a "historic preservation zone" and is radically closed to kayaks, canoes, boats and anything else that floats on the water. However, on any weekend you can see plenty of watercraft moving through this area. My assumption is that while the Park designated this section a historic zone, they do not have the ability to enforce that designation beyond their boundary. At any rate, if you kayak or canoe, you need to be aware that this restriction exists as the Park may find a way to enforce it in the future.

When the Millville gage reading is 3.0 ft or more, the main flow of the river moves hugs the east bank as it disperses over the staircase whose ridges stretch at a 45° angle away from the bridge. When the gage drops to 2.5 ft, the water runs down the west bank (Harpers Ferry side). It's not hard to figure out where the water is; all you have to do is watch the kayakers. They will always go where there is enough water to float their boat.

Some of the deeper sections are upstream on the Harpers Ferry side and you should enter the river near the bridge to move upstream so you can fish those spots from the center of the river. Given the ragged nature of the staircase, wading can be difficult or impossible at higher water levels. The farther upriver you go, the better the water becomes as it flows through and around various small islands that channel the water into deep cuts and runs. The rock structure here is spectacular and you can spend the entire day fishing the mile of water upstream. If you want to move from spot to spot quickly, use the rail bed that parallels the river all the way up to the quarry at Millville assuming the CSX railway has not posted it.

You might tempted to drive along the road leading from the parking lot to the visitor center that sits on a high bluff about a mile upriver. You are not allowed to park anywhere along the road; even if you could, a wide backwater blocks access to the river. Park below the bridge. It's a long walk down from the visitor center, but that is an option if you get desperate; although you still have to deal with crossing the swampy backwater.

While the best structure is in the mile immediately upstream of the bridge, you can also gain access to the Shenandoah from the town of Millville by following Bloomery Road along the river. Most of the small turnouts next to the river sport "posted" signs. The outfitters have major launching operations in picnic/park looking areas along the road and these are also posted as private property. There is public access near the dam at 39.275085,-77.786728. You can launch a canoe from there or wade if the water levels are good. Sometimes the outfitters will allow you to park in their areas for a fee.

Shoreline anglers will be disappointed with the staircase. They can move down from the bridge and fish the deep areas near the two rapids. Moving upstream, the close-in shoreline becomes a tangle of vegetation that will defeat anyone trying to work from the shore. The shoreline opens farther upstream near 39.317145,-77.74926 where the water deepens. You might be tempted to walk along the railroad tracks until the track swings back to the river near a rocky point, but, according to West Virginia law, railroad property is automatically considered to be posted unless the track is abandoned. There are exceptions for crossing tracks at public crossings such as the one from the parking lot to the river described above. So, your only choice is to wade and your next opportunity to fish a deep spot from the shore will be another mile farther up the river at 39.306559,-77.761493.

In terms of gear, both fly and spin anglers can use anything in their arsenal. Around the staircase and in some of the convoluted channels in the island area upstream from the bridge, fly anglers will have an advantage in that they will be able to use light poppers flipped up against the shore and next to the rocks. Spin anglers will have a hard time using crankbaits and other deep running lures. They should stick to grubs, tubes or weedless presentations.

This is the view up river across the staircase.

The Millville gage was running at 1.96 ft when this picture was taken.

The area near the shoreline is shallow and requires anglers to wade into the river.

Looking downstream from the bridge, the river runs across a shallow ledge until it hits the first of the two rapids.

The shoreline on the left is accessible, but the Park Service has signs posted asking people to stay on the trails to protect the environment.

At some point, the Park will probably restrict fishing from the bank so read all the signs to make sure you are legal.

Harpers Ferry City

Google Map Coordinates: 39.32682,-77.73497, 39.32812,-77.74092, 39.33268,-77.75038

Getting to the Stream

From US 340, turn onto Shenandoah Street. Follow Shenandoah Street all the way to the end. Pass by the bus depot where the Park Service drops off tourists; continue to the end and turn left on Potomac Street. You may be tempted to park on the right side of the street, but parking is limited to two hours. Continue up the street to the railroad station. There is plenty of parking, but it fills up with tourists. If you're willing to bounce on a rough dirt road, continue past the railroad tracks to reenter the Harpers Ferry National Historical Park and follow the road all the way up to the edge of Dam 3 (39.33231,-77.749804). A word of caution -- if you do not have a high clearance vehicle, you need to be careful since there are some deep erosion cuts across the road that might cause a normal vehicle to bottom out. There are a limited number of marginal places on the dirt road where you can park and walk over to the river; the best of the bad lot is at 39.32812,-77.74092.

There is a broad parking area on the left at the upper end of Potomac Street that looks inviting, but do not park there. That spot is for residents only. Beyond the railroad station, there are plenty of large, obvious signs warning that there is no parking beyond that point. I asked the Rangers if the signs applied the area beyond the railroad tracks and was told no; if you can find a space off the dirt road, you are welcome to park as long as you do not block the road. If you follow the road all the way up to Dam 3, there is room for five or six vehicles where it widens out near the water intake.

Beyond Dam 3, there is a camping area that is managed by a private company, but there are no signs preventing you from driving through to get to the National Park. In fact, if you hit the town during the height of the tourist season, you may want to use this northern approach to drive directly to Dam 3 without having to dodge around the crowds in town. To do that, from Rt 230, turn on Engles Switch Road (CR 29) and follow it across the railroad tracks until it dead ends at Bakerton Road (CR 28). Follow this road down to the river. Do not turn right to go over the railroad tracks. The road, although narrow, eventually drops you at the top of Dam 3. You can pick up Rt 230 in Shepherdstown or off of US 340 to the west of Harpers Ferry.

Hitting the river from Harpers Ferry puts you in the same place ("the needles") you would be if you drove west from Sandy Hook on the Maryland side. Therefore, I will not repeat the discussion of the water and refer you back to that chapter. I have one word of caution for those who drive up the dirt road to Dam 3. The water velocity is strong coming over the dam near the shore. You need to give the water the opportunity to spread out and lose energy as it disperses into the needles complex. Therefore, walk downstream to find a place to cross where the water is not intense.

The needles is a great area for fishing if you want to explore an almost infinite number of shallow channels that feed small holding pools. While the larger bass prefer pools that are deeper than 5 feet, the channels are full of sunfish and smaller bass that can be just as exciting to catch.

This is the view across the Dam 3 tailwater.

The rocks present a substantial obstacle to kayakers and a delight for anyone who is willing to wade.

The Point of Rocks gage was running at 1.68 ft when this picture was taken.

Another view looking downstream into the "needles."

There are some deeper holes near the cluster of trees at the right of this picture.

Otherwise, this section is a random collection of swiftly moving water that runs through narrow channels and collects in pools that are 2 to 3 feet deep.

There are not many options to reach the river from the narrow dirt road that leads up from the old power plant.

This picture shows the well defined vertical wall on the other side of the canal that parallels the dirt road. It is steep and represents a significant obstacle to overcome to reach the river. There are only a few places where you can park and find a place to climb safely over the wall.

The parking area next to the old power plant may or may not be open depending on the season and current park regulations when you arrive.

When you bump over the railroad tracks, you will see this to your right.

The only alternative to the parking congestion is to start early and claim a spot at the railroad station (39.32682,-77.73497).

You have to wade across a small backwater near the old power plant, crossing over Byrnes Island at the left, to get to the main river.

The Point of Rocks gage was running at 2.7 ft when this picture was taken and reflects a higher volume of water than is usually present.

Harpers Ferry Bottom line

The fact that it took so many pages to describe all the fishing options in this small location is ample proof that this is the perfect fishing destination for any angler. Your biggest challenge will be dealing with all of the other people who use this area for hiking, biking, boating and the normal tourism that occurs at a historic site. The universal solution is to arrive early in the day and grab a parking spot.

Potomac Bass Fishing Clubs

New Horizon Bass Anglers

New Horizon Bass Anglers

Meets at the
Neighbor's Sports Bar & Restaurant
262D Cedar Lane (at Park St.)
Vienna, Va.

2nd Thursday of each month

Website
www.nhbayouthfoundation.org

The New Horizon Bass Anglers is a bass fishing club centered in the Northern Virginia area. Its members come from Virginia, Maryland, Washington DC, and other nearby jurisdictions.

The club fishes a wide array of lakes and rivers including the Potomac, Lake Anna, James River, Rappahannock River, Lake Gaston, Buggs Island, Smith Mountain Lake and more.

The club is a fellowship of bass anglers committed to having fun through fishing. It exists to help members improve their fishing knowledge and skills through practical application on sponsored events as well as sharing information at club meetings. A primary goal of the club is to develop camaraderie as each member helps others become better anglers. The club recognizes the importance of friendly competition and sponsors a number of bass tournaments to provide another venue to put people on the water and have fun.

The club is also committed to conservation and protection of the fisheries resource, not only in thoughts and actions, but with financial assistance as well.

A particular passion of the club is to sponsor youth fishing derbies for kids ages 15 and under during the summer months.

Typically, the club holds these free events at Lake Fairfax in Reston. The derbies provide kids an introduction to the sport of fishing as well as an overview of related conservation topics. Professional guides attend these events to respond to questions and inject their experienced perspective.

Kids do not need to have a fishing license to participate. While the club prefers everyone bring their own rod and reel that is not a barrier to participation. The club has loaner equipment that it provides at these events.

The term and schedule for the club is designed to keep everyone on the water! Nominally, the club sponsors 15 tournaments during the course of the year but the number may be adjusted based on conditions. The tournament activities culminate in a "classic tournament" at year's end. Each tournament has a small prize for the winners funded out of the $10 entry fee.

The club's website includes a discussion forum focused on fishing the water that is local to the Washington Metropolitan area. It includes discussion of tips and techniques, lures and other topics.

The material in this section was paraphrased or directly quoted from the NBHA website.

Potomac River Smallmouth Club

Potomac River Smallmouth Club

Meets at the Vienna Fire Station 400 Center Street South

Last Wednesday of each month

Website
www.prsc.org

"The Potomac River Smallmouth Club (PRSC) is the Washington D.C. Capital Area's leading river fishing and conservation organization. We promote **catch and release** angling for smallmouth bass, support conservation organizations and agencies, publish a monthly newsletter, present monthly programs with guest speakers, and organize frequent river trips for our members. While we are principally focused on smallmouth bass fishing in the Potomac River watershed, we also sponsor trips to other destinations such the Shenandoah, James, New, Cacapon and Susquehanna.

The PRSC was founded in 1988 as a non-profit recreational club in accordance with IRS section 501(c)(7). While concentrating our efforts on the improvement of smallmouth bass fishing in the region's rivers, PRSC supports the preservation of fish habitat and the wise management of all river gamefish species. The Club emphasizes knowledge of safe boating and wading skills as central to an enjoyable river experience. PRSC participates in various community sporting activities including:

- Safe use of canoes, kayaks and other river watercraft
- River cleanup
- Advocacy for environmental issues affecting water quality, aquatic habitat and fisheries management
- Annual fishing contest
- Recreational and educational events for young people, veterans and other groups
- Equipment demonstrations and new product evaluation

The PRSC works closely with state and federal agencies, other membership organizations and various businesses on matters of common interest."

-       Quoted from the PRSC web site

Joining the club is easy. Just show up! Meetings are open to the public and annual membership, as of 2010, is only $35. Membership allows you to participate in the wide variety of events the club sponsors.

One of the great benefits of membership is "The Buzz", the monthly newsletter of the club. Content varies month to month and typically includes information on club meetings and events.

The newsletter is the vehicle the club uses to discuss and address conservation issues, disseminate safety information and announces the much anticipated fishing contest standings.

All members of the club are encouraged to write and submit articles for publication.

The club sponsors many trips to all of the top smallmouth bass fishing destinations within a reasonable distance of the Washington DC metro area.

The great benefit of going with a group is the ability to provide shuttle for canoes and kayaks as well as leverage the hundreds of years of fishing experience of the membership that puts the trip on the right place at the right time for top action.

For more information on the club and how to join, visit their website at www.prsc.org or send an e-mail to president@prsc.org.

Note: The meeting schedule varies from the last Wednesday during October thru December. Contact the club to confirm the schedule if you decide to attend a meeting scheduled during those months.

This section was developed using material that was either quoted or paraphrased from the PRSC website. However, the author is a member of this club.

Guides

Mark Kovach Fishing Services

Mark Kovach Fishing Services

406 Pershing Drive
Silver Spring, MD 20910
(301) 588-8742

Mark Kovach
Owner

Website
www.mkfs.com

Since 1979, Mark and his team have provided a unique fishing service by specializing in putting their customers on the best bass water of the Upper Potomac -- the stretch protected by the churning rapids that turn the river to a boil in the 8 miles between Harpers Ferry and Brunswick Maryland.

"I want to caution you from the onset that this stretch of the Potomac River is considered one of the most hazardous on the river…. Only experienced canoeists should attempt the float but if you are looking for a fun-filled fishing trip, do as I do and hire Mark Kovach, who has assembled a team of excellent fishing guides."

- Ken Penrod in "Fishing the Upper Potomac River"

For three decades, Mark's specially designed boats, the *Iron Maiden* and *Potomac Mistress,* have been the secret weapon he uses to move countless enthusiastic anglers through the Class III whitewater bordering deep pools punctuated by dramatic ledges and random islands.

"If I could design and construct a 400 yard stretch of bass habitat, I'd copy this area."
- Ken Penrod on the section that Mark fishes from "Fishing the Upper Potomac River"

According to Mark, to adapt to the unique characteristics of this wild stretch of the river, he customized 14 1/2-foot inflatable whitewater rafts and equipped them with custom-made aluminum frames. Mark indicates that "Swivel bucket seats, chain drag and anchoring systems, fishing rod storage racks, coolers stocked with food and drinks, and other special features" round out the package to provide his customers a comfortable, easy fishing experience.

The float trips include a full day of instruction in fishing and launch from above Dam three around 8:00 AM in the morning. Your trip will end at Brunswick at dusk. The trip includes either fly or spin gear along with the seasonally appropriate mix of flies and lures. His guides are skilled at reading the water, communicating with customers, and are happy to share their wealth of knowledge of the history, geology and river lore that makes this stretch of the Upper Potomac one of the most interesting.

Mark conducts fly fishing schools on selected Saturdays between April and the end of September. During the spring, the school centers on providing basic and intermediate instruction for trout using Big Hunting Creek in Thurmont, MD as the classroom. In the summer, the action switches to bass with focused schools hosted in the Potomac at Harpers Ferry. Mark can conduct advanced bass schools that include video analysis of your casting style and schedules them based on interest.

 Of course, private instruction is available with rates per hour and special dates can be arranged for groups.

Mark participates in a number of fishing shows between January and March each year to include the Rapidan TU Show in Middleburg as well as the National Capital Angling Show held in the DC area. Be sure and check in with him if you happen to be at any of those events.

The Angler's Inn - Guide Service, B&B and Fly Shop

The Angler's Inn

867 W. Washington Street
Harpers Ferry, WV 25425
(304) 535-1239

Bryan Kelly
Owner

Website
http:theanglersinn.com

Bryan Kelly and his wife, Debbi, operate the only "triple threat" on the Upper Potomac. They can put you up for the night, outfit you with everything you need and then pop you into a handcrafted, western-style McKenzie drift boat or a fully rigged NRS Whitewater raft for a day you'll never forget. You may have read about their unique operation in the Baltimore Sun, Washington Post, Chesapeake Angler, Woods and Water, Shenandoah Valley Review, Fly Fish America, Virginia Outdoorsman or seen the 8 page center spread in Eastern Fly Fishing magazine. Words can only communicate so much - especially when written by others who may have different priorities than you. You need to visit the Angler's Inn and fish with them to create a permanent, warm memory that will compel you to return time and time again.

The Angler's Inn Bed and Breakfast is located on the main street of historic Harpers Ferry just steps away from over 100 years of history. Opened in 1997, the Kelly's have fully restored an old Victorian home to provide all of the modern conveniences yet retain the architectural integrity of the original 1880 building. While not required, a stay in the Bed and Breakfast provides the perfect start for your day on the water. Choose either the full gourmet breakfast that will stick with you all day or opt for the lighter continental fare to move quickly to the business at hand - fishing!

Once on the water, Bryan's 20 years of experience as a guide comes into play as he puts you at the right place at the right time. Bryan demands the same level of dedication, intuition, customer service and "river smarts" from all of the guides who work for him. The team works the Potomac River from Dam 4 all the way down to the Point of Rocks. While you can't make that long trip in a single day, Bryan will work with you to develop the right itinerary that takes advantage of the current river conditions.

If you prefer to fish the main stem of the Shenandoah, Bryan's team of guides is equally skilled in outsmarting smallmouth bass on that river as well.

The choice between the Potomac and Shenandoah tough to make. In 2005, Fly Fisherman Magazine ranked both rivers in the top 10 in the country for taking smallmouth bass on surface flies. However, do not feel that you have to be a fly fisherman to take advantage of the guide service. The Angler's guide team is equally at home with spinning gear.

The McKenzie drift boat and the NRS Whitewater rafts are set up to handle two anglers and all their gear for a full day of fishing. The trips typically run eight hours and include guide, boat, fly outfits, flies, spinning tackle, lures, lunch, and beverages. Check the website for current pricing and be sure to review the special packages that blend fishing with overnight stays at the Inn.

The last element of the triple threat is Kelly's White Fly Shop located on the main street of Shepherdstown. Kelly's carries a full line of flies, brand name rods, reels, clothing and gear sure to make all your fly fishing experiences more enjoyable. Bryan personally hand selects gear and accessories from companies with earned reputations for designing quality products for anglers. You will find Abel Reels, St. Croix Rods, Royal Wulff Line, Fishpond, Patagonia, and Renzetti on the shelf and ready to go.

The White Fly Shop Is the only operation of its kind within a reasonable distance of this end of the Upper Potomac. If you are a beginning fly angler or just need to tune up your fly fishing technique, the shop sponsors two hour casting clinics on weekday evenings in the Spring, Summer and Fall. They fill up fast since Dusty Wissmath, a world-class fly casting instructor, teaches many of them himself. Call ahead to get the detailed schedule; they are first-come, first-served.

Bryan participates in a number of the area's premier fly fishing tradeshows. You can usually see him at the Somerset NJ Fly Show, the Charlotte show, the Arundel Mills Bass Pro Shops Spring Classic as well as at other major events such as the Virginia Fly Fishing Festival.

Ken Penrod's Life Outdoors Unlimited

Life Outdoors Unlimited
Guide Service
4708 Sellman Road
Beltsville, MD 20705
(301) 937-0010

Ken Penrod
Owner

Website
www.penrodsguides.com

Ken Penrod is so well known, and name so tightly linked to smallmouth bass fishing on the Potomac, that if you mention his name while on the water, you will spook the fish.

Ken Penrod (email: kenpenrod@comcast.net) has been in the business for over 28 years and his guide service, Life Outdoors Unlimited, is one of the best-known operations on the Potomac. Consisting of over a dozen guides, this service covers most of the waters in Maryland, Delaware, District of Columbia, Virginia and Pennsylvania. In addition to smallmouth bass, his team of experts can put you on the largemouth, striped bass, catfish or even crappie.

Life Outdoors Unlimited only hires professional guides. As a result of this, they are the "go to" experts relied on by the entire range of anglers from professionals to those new to the sport. However, celebrity is not an advantage since the guide team approaches every day with the same level of professionalism and enthusiasm focused on a single goal -- find fish. The service operates 12 months a year, seven days a week and offers half day, full day as well as overnight expeditions.

If you have more people than will fit in a single boat, the operation has the capability to surge and dedicate several craft to your event. In fact, their largest event involved 50 boats. The service prefers that you provide your own rods, reels and tackle but will provide gear for you if requested. The service welcomes fly anglers but will not loan fly rods; you must bring your own. The office will run through these as well as other details, such as the current rates, when you call to coordinate your trip.

If you have more people than will fit in a single boat, the operation has the capability to surge and dedicate several craft to your event. In fact, the largest event today guided involved 50 boats. The service prefers that you provide your own rods, reels and tackle but will provide gear for you if requested. The service welcomes fly anglers but will not loan fly rods; you must bring your own. The office will run through these as well as other details, such as the current rates, when you call to coordinate your trip.

Outdoor Life Unlimited welcomes children and enjoys introducing them to fishing. Ken's commitment to kids extends to his summer youth camp, Camp Sycamore, located outside of Sinnamahoning, Pennsylvania. The camp allows 6 to 8 boys between the ages of 12 and 17 to attend weeklong sessions that run from mid-July to mid-August. When you look at the camp's program that includes wade fishing in a Susquehanna tributary, fishing from bass boats on reservoirs, stalking small creeks with fly gear for brook and rainbow trout, map reading, shooting and a host of other outdoor activities, you can't help but wish that you were a kid again so you could go. Unfortunately, there is no adult version of this program.

As a nationally recognized expert, Ken's organization is sponsored by the "first string" of gear manufacturers such as Lowrance, Mercury, Ranger, Minn Kota and others. This gives his team an inside track on the latest in technology; all shared with you during your day on the water.

Beyond the guide service, Ken is a prolific author who shares his expertise in four acclaimed books. In fact, *Fishing the Upper Potomac River* was the inspiration for this book.

Ken's most recent book, *Pursuing River Smallmouth Bass*, is 156 pages of information I wish I knew 40 years ago. If you only can buy one other book to go with this one, get it. The book provides the smallmouth bass "smarts" -- the techniques and tactics -- that will allow you to have a great day in any of the places discussed in this volume.

All of Ken Penrod's books are available for $25 from:

PPC Publications
4708 Sellman Road
Beltsville, MD 20705
(301) 937-0010

Price includes priority mailing.

Ken's books include:

- Fishing the Upper Potomac River
- Ken Penrod's Tidal Potomac River Fishing Bible
- Ken Penrod's Top Ten For Fishing PAMARVA
- Pursuing River Smallmouth Bass

You can download an order form from Ken's website.

Mean (Average) Gage Height in Feet for Key Gages

Point of Rocks gage Height:

Day	Jan	Feb	Mar	Apr	May	Jun	Jul	Aug	Sep	Oct	Nov	Dec
	Gage height in Feet											
	Daily mean values for each day for 8 years of record											
1	3.25	2.97	3.57	4.85	4.63	3.07	2.44	2.17	1.68	3.35	2.99	4.71
2	3.65	3.03	3.74	4.79	4.24	3.05	2.19	2.2	1.72	2.82	2.71	4.08
3	4.71	3.07	4.6	5.43	4.17	2.94	2.04	2.02	2.07	2.52	2.47	3.51
4	4.49	3.09	4.93	5.28	4.1	3.28	1.98	1.81	2.27	2.31	2.3	3.23
5	4.15	3.07	4.54	4.75	3.87	3.92	2.05	1.75	2.38	2.18	2.18	3.16
6	3.88	3.21	5.64	4.34	3.64	3.79	1.99	1.75	2.33	2.09	2.15	2.99
7	3.9	3.51	6.06	4.06	3.57	3.69	2.08	1.75	2.19	2.06	2.23	2.85
8	3.83	4.13	5.66	3.95	3.43	3.95	2.27	1.69	1.94	2.22	2.45	2.72
9	3.73	3.88	5.36	4.28	3.36	3.86	2.17	1.68	1.91	2.52	2.58	2.65
10	3.77	3.49	5.42	4.45	3.56	3.45	2.23	1.63	2.91	2.44	2.72	2.7
11	3.56	3.3	5.07	4.56	4.12	3.12	2.34	1.6	2.47	2.31	2.63	3.81
12	3.43	3.21	4.55	4.77	5.26	2.84	2.14	1.73	2.13	2.11	2.56	5.65
13	3.73	3.12	4.26	5.11	5.41	2.77	2.01	1.94	1.99	2.07	2.96	5.11
14	3.87	3	4.19	5.63	4.59	3.16	1.97	2.1	1.92	2.05	3.6	4.63
15	3.84	3.04	4.28	5.63	3.99	3.16	1.92	2.11	1.89	2.03	3.73	4.71
16	3.79	3.04	4.23	6.18	4.09	2.98	1.9	1.92	1.82	2.01	3.07	4.54
17	3.55	3.09	4.3	6.27	4.78	2.87	1.94	1.8	1.76	2.12	3.23	4.24
18	3.3	3.08	4.41	5.35	4.5	2.78	1.95	1.75	2.21	2.41	4.45	4.1
19	3.22	3.08	4.27	4.79	4.3	2.77	1.86	1.64	3.35	2.32	4.16	3.92
20	3.38	3.03	4.32	4.57	4.67	2.72	1.87	1.6	4.67	2.2	4.06	3.62
21	3.3	3.1	5.41	4.65	4.47	2.78	1.74	1.61	4.23	2.14	4.76	3.38
22	3.22	3.4	6.86	5.2	4.44	3.05	1.69	1.75	3	2.09	4.12	3.39
23	3.07	4.03	6.67	5.4	4.43	2.94	1.73	2.01	3.08	1.97	3.78	3.45
24	2.99	5.02	5.93	5.91	4.16	2.92	1.7	1.73	3.32	1.9	3.67	3.44
25	2.94	4.7	5.62	5.2	4.1	2.67	1.68	1.66	2.83	1.93	3.59	3.83
26	2.83	4.1	5.13	4.72	3.78	2.6	1.7	1.63	2.43	1.96	3.61	4.06
27	2.72	3.79	4.68	4.99	3.57	2.55	1.69	1.6	2.25	2.1	3.37	3.95
28	2.66	3.67	4.52	5.15	3.66	2.97	1.62	1.6	2.4	2.32	3.19	3.81
29	2.55	4.12	5.1	4.9	3.51	3.17	1.71	1.64	3.53	2.65	3.33	3.64
30	2.54		5.74	5.11	3.33	2.76	1.99	1.65	4.29	2.71	3.77	3.46
31	2.59		5.21		3.22		1.95	1.68		2.85		3.43

Little Falls Gage Height:

	Gage height in feet											
	Daily mean values for each day for 8 years of record											
Day	Jan	Feb	Mar	Apr	May	Jun	Jul	Aug	Sep	Oct	Nov	Dec
1	3.92	3.73	4.10	4.74	4.67	3.90	3.56	3.17	2.93	3.80	3.54	4.27
2	4.17	3.92	4.17	4.74	4.46	3.84	3.42	3.26	2.99	3.53	3.51	4.19
3	4.46	3.91	4.48	5.03	4.39	3.82	3.32	3.26	3.01	3.36	3.41	3.98
4	4.46	3.92	4.67	4.98	4.37	3.87	3.29	3.14	3.16	3.27	3.34	3.84
5	4.33	3.94	4.56	4.73	4.24	4.22	3.33	3.06	3.35	3.20	3.30	3.76
6	4.21	3.95	4.85	4.53	4.14	4.26	3.37	3.03	3.35	3.16	3.33	3.68
7	4.18	4.21	5.12	4.39	4.06	4.25	3.32	3.01	3.33	3.15	3.29	3.61
8	4.23	4.30	5.04	4.31	4.04	4.24	3.57	3.00	3.16	3.32	3.38	3.57
9	4.19	4.24	4.90	4.38	4.02	4.25	3.56	2.98	3.03	3.34	3.46	3.53
10	4.11	4.06	4.89	4.47	4.04	4.05	3.41	2.97	3.24	3.32	3.44	3.56
11	4.04	3.97	4.79	4.54	4.19	3.89	3.43	2.99	3.35	3.26	3.45	4.09
12	3.99	3.91	4.56	4.59	4.87	3.80	3.37	3.07	3.14	3.20	3.46	4.61
13	4.01	3.90	4.41	4.85	4.96	3.77	3.29	3.06	3.05	3.14	3.59	4.59
14	4.28	3.86	4.35	5.00	4.63	3.83	3.29	3.06	3.01	3.12	3.77	4.38
15	4.29	3.81	4.36	5.06	4.33	3.90	3.31	3.12	3.01	3.18	3.86	4.34
16	4.17	3.84	4.40	5.12	4.37	3.86	3.27	3.07	2.97	3.20	3.87	4.42
17	4.09	3.81	4.44	5.26	4.59	3.72	3.25	3.05	2.93	3.16	3.91	4.42
18	3.74	3.82	4.44	4.96	4.60	3.70	3.25	2.99	2.97	3.22	4.11	4.47
19	4.00	3.83	4.39	4.67	4.40	3.74	3.21	2.92	3.64	3.25	4.10	4.26
20	4.01	3.83	4.40	4.57	4.55	3.71	3.16	2.92	3.99	3.26	4.10	4.14
21	4.04	3.88	4.81	4.67	4.59	3.65	3.14	2.90	4.03	3.20	4.21	4.02
22	3.88	4.04	5.36	4.81	4.50	3.71	3.07	2.87	3.53	3.18	4.11	3.92
23	3.89	4.37	5.52	4.78	4.51	3.83	3.10	2.94	3.64	3.17	3.99	3.96
24	3.78	4.60	5.32	5.12	4.40	3.70	3.14	2.98	3.79	3.12	3.90	4.05
25	3.80	4.63	5.10	4.93	4.40	3.67	3.11	2.91	3.69	3.18	3.87	4.11
26	3.72	4.38	4.87	4.66	4.30	3.79	3.06	2.85	3.39	3.23	3.91	4.19
27	3.70	4.22	4.67	4.68	4.19	3.70	3.08	2.86	3.30	3.32	3.87	4.16
28	3.56	4.19	4.59	4.90	4.10	3.78	3.10	2.88	3.25	3.41	3.78	4.07
29	3.60	4.32	4.78	4.74	4.10	3.89	3.06	2.92	3.73	3.52	3.73	4.01
30	3.60		5.07	4.75	4.00	3.73	3.09	2.90	4.03	3.57	3.94	3.94
31	3.64		4.95		3.92		3.17	2.90		3.50		3.90

Median Gage Height

To revisit high school math, the median value is the value that is the middle value in the data set while the mean that is the average of all the values. When planning, the median is a better measure to use since it mitigates the impact of severe floods or droughts that pull the mean value up or down.

Little Falls - Median

Median Gage height in Feet											
Median of daily mean values for each day for 8 years of record											
Day	Jan	Feb	Mar	Apr	May	Jun	Jul	Aug	Sep	Oct	Nov	Dec
1	4.17	3.58	3.96	4.42	4.19	3.83	3.26	3.08	2.87	2.9	3.39	4.04
2	4.15	3.68	3.92	4.67	4.12	3.67	3.23	3	2.91	2.91	3.44	3.96
3	4.14	3.67	3.9	4.69	4.2	3.6	3.18	2.91	2.9	2.89	3.5	3.88
4	4.1	3.77	3.86	4.64	4.24	3.54	3.19	2.91	2.84	2.91	3.55	3.81
5	4.05	3.84	4	4.59	4.14	3.46	3.21	2.9	2.8	2.9	3.63	3.76
6	4.06	3.93	4.73	4.47	4.1	3.54	3.25	2.91	2.84	2.8	3.59	3.7
7	4.28	3.85	4.67	4.35	4.09	3.79	3.22	2.93	2.83	2.88	3.52	3.63
8	4.65	3.83	4.6	4.25	3.97	3.74	3.54	2.91	2.84	3.31	3.89	3.62
9	4.57	3.8	4.65	4.23	3.88	3.8	3.46	2.95	2.84	3.77	3.98	3.56
10	4.36	3.79	4.83	4.2	3.9	3.68	3.4	2.95	2.85	3.68	3.86	3.52
11	4.24	3.81	4.86	4.21	4.01	3.62	3.38	2.92	2.79	3.6	3.77	3.55
12	4.2	3.8	4.73	4.21	3.91	3.54	3.34	2.92	2.77	3.48	3.91	3.62
13	4.2	3.83	4.68	4.39	3.85	3.46	3.28	2.91	2.76	3.28	4.01	3.99
14	4.31	3.84	4.55	4.37	3.8	3.46	3.36	2.92	2.76	3.18	4.12	3.96
15	4.25	3.89	4.38	4.57	3.78	3.42	3.37	2.91	2.79	3.15	4.26	3.87
16	4.14	3.96	4.26	4.69	3.82	3.45	3.33	2.87	2.77	3.31	4.28	4.36
17	4.01	4.09	4.21	4.72	3.99	3.38	3.26	2.84	2.76	3.29	4.14	4.68
18	3.85	4.14	4.16	4.6	4.02	3.43	3.21	2.83	2.73	3.41	4.03	4.48
19	3.91	4.16	4.15	4.49	4.02	3.42	3.13	2.84	2.71	3.39	3.95	4.35
20	3.88	4.12	4.25	4.41	4.4	3.27	3.12	2.91	2.7	3.38	3.9	4.23
21	3.87	4.04	4.63	4.68	4.47	3.16	3.09	2.95	2.76	3.42	3.83	4.09
22	3.77	4.02	5.1	4.57	4.22	3.15	3.02	2.94	2.72	3.49	3.78	3.9
23	3.88	4.02	5.2	4.53	4.24	3.22	3.05	3.02	2.69	3.37	3.86	3.74
24	3.7	3.98	5.34	4.71	4.32	3.16	3.16	3.03	2.64	3.23	3.83	4.17
25	3.71	3.95	5.31	4.61	4.49	3.37	3.19	2.95	2.89	3.3	3.86	4.16
26	3.63	3.95	5	4.5	4.39	3.45	3.22	2.88	2.87	3.25	4.32	4.3
27	3.66	3.91	4.77	4.57	4.28	3.43	3.21	2.85	2.96	3.22	4.16	4.26
28	3.48	4	4.59	4.63	4.18	3.38	3.2	2.86	2.88	3.45	4.02	4.13
29	3.55	4.32	4.44	4.4	4.11	3.34	3.12	2.88	3.04	3.42	3.58	4.28
30	3.58		4.5	4.28	4.02	3.36	3.04	2.84	3.09	3.53	4.13	4.15
31	3.56		4.34		3.99		3.15	2.85		3.4		4.1

Point of Rocks Median Gage Height

	Median Gage height in feet											
	Median of daily mean values for each day for 8 years of record											
Day	Jan	Feb	Mar	Apr	May	Jun	Jul	Aug	Sep	Oct	Nov	Dec
1	3.48	2.54	3.29	4.16	3.56	2.91	1.89	1.79	1.58	1.7	2.38	3.3
2	3.48	2.62	3.26	4.63	3.52	2.64	1.78	1.83	1.92	1.68	2.52	3.13
3	3.55	2.58	3.2	4.71	3.83	2.44	1.75	1.75	1.84	1.67	2.56	2.89
4	3.28	2.69	3.09	4.65	3.69	2.29	1.75	1.69	1.78	1.72	2.45	2.79
5	3.39	2.67	3.54	4.47	3.5	2.42	1.78	1.72	1.72	1.54	2.48	2.77
6	3.43	3.13	4.92	4.22	3.54	2.39	1.77	1.89	1.96	1.49	2.51	2.62
7	4.29	3	4.67	3.96	3.58	2.55	1.95	1.74	1.86	1.6	2.36	2.58
8	4.39	2.88	4.56	3.84	3.34	3.13	2.38	1.59	1.75	1.92	2.61	2.48
9	4.38	2.82	4.86	3.88	3.24	2.83	2.2	1.53	1.67	2.14	3.1	2.38
10	4.09	2.79	5.26	3.93	3.18	2.59	2.24	1.54	1.75	2.5	3.27	2.39
11	3.78	2.85	5.09	3.83	3.28	2.45	2.08	1.57	1.76	2.48	3.08	2.49
12	3.6	3.02	4.91	3.77	3.17	2.31	1.98	1.6	1.79	1.95	3.07	3.29
13	4.04	3.12	4.8	3.8	3.04	2.23	1.93	1.63	1.88	2.24	3.25	4.17
14	3.88	3.08	4.49	4.15	2.93	2.21	1.92	1.72	1.88	2.53	3.73	3.75
15	3.8	3.17	4.12	4.05	2.94	2.14	1.81	1.68	1.94	2.31	4.2	4.22
16	3.77	3.14	3.98	4.67	3.04	2.08	1.91	1.61	1.93	2.09	2.85	4.75
17	3.55	3.39	3.87	5.01	3.62	2.26	1.9	1.66	1.85	2.03	2.82	4.53
18	3.32	3.74	3.86	4.67	3.58	2.23	1.73	1.65	1.84	2.19	3.58	4.49
19	3.17	3.7	3.95	4.32	4	2.02	1.72	1.52	1.82	2.29	3.47	4.47
20	3.05	3.56	4.3	4.57	4.56	1.86	1.73	1.53	1.77	2.34	3.33	4.18
21	2.92	3.39	4.83	4.76	4.12	1.74	1.55	1.53	1.72	2.52	3.23	3.83
22	3	3.32	6.6	4.47	3.79	1.81	1.53	1.75	1.68	2.49	3.39	3.36
23	2.89	3.38	6.02	4.95	4.12	1.81	1.62	1.86	1.63	2.28	3.49	3.1
24	2.64	3.25	5.65	4.86	4.06	1.76	1.69	1.63	1.6	2.12	3.4	3.01
25	2.58	3.21	6.16	4.62	4.17	1.85	1.78	1.52	1.62	2.01	3.61	3.51
26	2.57	3.19	5.56	4.65	4.14	2.37	1.76	1.42	1.51	2.11	4.34	3.75
27	2.51	3.21	5.05	4.61	4	2.23	1.73	1.34	1.5	2.19	3.99	4
28	2.41	3.33	4.63	4.24	3.68	2.14	1.7	1.3	1.7	2.53	3.65	3.65
29	2.39	4.12	4.29	3.98	3.57	2.02	1.67	1.29	2.05	2.54	3.49	3.85
30	2.45		4.27	3.76	3.44	1.93	1.73	1.43	2.42	2.81	3.48	3.61
31	2.43		4.11		3.24		1.74	1.66		2.56		3.5

Mean (Average) Water Temperature

This data is only available for the Little Falls gage. Based on this, it is warm enough to wet wade between mid-June and mid-September.

	Water Temperature in degrees Fahrenheit											
	Daily mean values for each day for 9 years of record											
Day	Jan	Feb	Mar	Apr	May	Jun	Jul	Aug	Sep	Oct	Nov	Dec
1	39.2	36.3	41.2	52.9	62.6	74.8	83.1	85.5	80.1	67.1	54.3	47.8
2	39.2	36.5	41.7	54.0	63.7	75.6	83.8	86.0	78.3	66.9	54.5	46.9
3	39.0	36.7	41.9	54.5	64.2	74.5	83.8	86.5	78.3	67.6	54.3	45.5
4	39.4	37.0	42.1	54.1	64.0	73.6	83.8	86.0	78.6	68.5	54.7	44.2
5	39.9	36.7	43.5	53.4	64.2	73.2	83.8	85.6	78.1	68.9	53.6	43.3
6	40.3	36.7	43.7	53.2	64.6	73.2	83.8	84.7	76.8	68.4	53.8	42.1
7	39.9	36.9	44.1	54.0	65.1	74.1	83.8	84.9	76.5	67.3	53.1	41.7
8	40.1	37.0	45.0	54.0	65.8	75.6	83.1	84.4	76.8	66.7	52.7	41.4
9	40.1	37.4	45.0	53.8	66.2	76.8	83.1	83.8	77.2	66.6	51.8	41.0
10	39.6	37.6	45.7	54.7	66.9	77.7	83.5	83.1	77.4	66.2	51.3	41.0
11	39.0	37.8	46.0	55.6	67.6	77.9	83.5	82.8	76.6	65.1	51.1	41.5
12	39.2	37.4	46.2	56.1	67.5	78.3	83.8	82.9	75.9	64.2	51.1	41.2
13	39.6	37.0	46.6	56.3	67.5	78.3	83.7	83.1	75.6	63.7	50.5	41.4
14	40.6	36.9	47.8	56.7	67.1	77.9	83.5	83.3	75.9	63.1	50.2	41.0
15	39.7	37.6	48.6	57.4	67.3	78.1	82.9	83.3	75.7	62.8	50.7	40.8
16	38.7	37.9	48.7	58.8	68.0	77.9	83.7	83.1	75.6	61.9	51.6	41.0
17	37.6	38.3	48.0	59.5	68.2	77.7	84.6	82.6	75.6	61.0	51.6	40.8
18	37.2	38.3	47.3	59.5	67.6	79.2	85.3	82.0	75.2	60.6	50.7	40.6
19	36.0	37.9	47.3	60.4	66.6	80.2	86.7	81.9	74.1	60.8	50.4	40.6
20	35.4	38.3	47.7	61.5	65.1	80.2	86.2	81.7	73.0	60.6	50.0	39.9
21	34.9	38.8	47.3	61.9	64.6	80.1	85.5	81.3	73.0	60.4	49.3	39.2
22	34.5	39.7	46.9	61.2	64.9	79.9	85.1	81.3	72.9	59.9	49.1	39.0
23	34.7	40.3	47.1	60.6	66.0	80.2	84.4	81.5	72.7	59.4	48.2	40.3
24	35.1	40.1	48.0	61.0	67.3	80.6	83.5	81.3	72.7	58.5	47.7	40.6
25	35.1	40.5	49.3	60.6	68.2	81.5	83.1	81.7	72.3	57.4	47.3	39.9
26	34.7	40.8	50.2	60.8	69.4	81.9	82.8	81.9	71.8	56.8	46.8	39.2
27	34.9	40.8	50.7	61.3	70.3	82.0	82.8	81.3	71.6	56.7	46.9	38.8
28	35.2	40.6	51.1	61.3	70.3	82.2	82.4	81.0	71.6	56.3	48.4	38.1
29	35.8	43.2	51.8	61.5	70.7	83.1	83.1	80.6	70.7	55.0	48.0	38.3
30	36.5	32.0	52.2	61.7	72.0	83.5	83.8	80.8	69.3	54.1	48.0	38.3
31	36.9		52.3		73.2		84.7	80.8		54.1		38.5

Made in the USA
Lexington, KY
27 February 2011